11 AFRICAN AMERICAN DOCTORS

11 AFRICAN AMERICAN DOCTORS

Robert C. Hayden

Twenty-First Century Books

A Division of Henry Holt and Company
New York

Twenty-First Century Books
A Division of Henry Holt and Company, Inc.
115 West 18th Street
New York, NY 10011

Henry Holt® and colophon are trademarks of Henry Holt and Company, Inc.
Publishers since 1866

Published in Canada by Fitzhenry & Whiteside Ltd.,
195 Allstate Parkway, Markham, Ontario L3R 4T8.

Cover photo by Richard Laird/FPG International
Portrait illustrations by Richard Loehle

Library of Congress Cataloging-in-Publication Data

Hayden, Robert C.
11 African-American Doctors
Illustrated by Richard Loehle

Includes index.

Summary: Chronicles the achievements of eleven Afro-American
physicians whose contributions helped raise the country's health
standards through medical practice, research, or teaching.

1. Afro-American physicians—Biography—Juvenile literature.
[1. Physicians.   2. Afro-Americans—Biography.]   I. Loehle, Richard,
ill.   II. Title.   III. Title: Eleven African-American doctors.   IV. Title:
African-American doctors.   V. Series: Hayden, Robert C., Achievers:
African Americans in Science and Technology.

R695.H39   1992   610.92'273—dc20   [B]   91-44195   CIP   AC
ISBN 0-8050-2135-3

First Edition—1970

Printed in Mexico
All first editions are printed on acid-free paper.

10 9 8 7 6

CONTENTS

FOREWORD

This book is dedicated to all young people who aspire to careers in medicine.

This book could not have been written without the help of relatives, friends, and associates of the eleven doctors. Most important were the interviews and resource materials provided by the doctors themselves. There were institutions, too, that were helpful in providing vital resource materials. I sincerely thank the following people and institutions for their interest and sharing of memories and information:

Individuals: Dr. and Mrs. Eugene Adams, Dr. Farrow Allen, Mr. Charles Alston, Dr. George Cannon, Dr. Kenneth Clark, the late Dr. William Montague Cobb, Carolyn Cobb Wilkenson, Amelia Cobb-Gray, Mr. Charles Collins, Dr. and Mrs. Daniel Collins, Miss Louise Crowd, Dr. Leon Cruise, Dr. Angella Ferguson, Mrs. Harriet Fuller, Mr. Solomon C. Fuller, Jr., the late Mr. Thomas W. Fuller, Dr. Kenneth Girard, Miss Frances Grant, Dr. Joseph Henry, Dr. Jane Hinton, Mr. Charles Jones, Mrs. Marian Logan, Dr. Myra Logan, Dr. Thomas W. Patrick, Jr., Dr. Charles Pinderhughes, the late Judge Francis Ellis Rivers, Judge G. Bruce Robinson, Miss Genevieve Stuart, Dr. William Walker, Dr. Jane Wright, Mrs. Louis T. Wright.

Institutions: Atlanta Public Library, the Francis A. Countway Library of Medicine, Hartford Public Library, Howard University Medical Library, *The Interpreter* published by the United Methodist Church, *Journal of the National Medical Association,* New York Academy of Medicine, Office of Informational Services of the Boston University Medical Center, University of Connecticut Medical Center Library.

A special thanks to Evelyn and Mary Noonan and Deborah Hayden for their youthful editorial input, to Delores Noonan and Rosalind Savage for typing services, to Aileen and Stephen Davis for research advice and help, to Dr. Willis N. Cummings for information on the Badger brothers, and to William H. Hayden for providing a home away from home on research trips to New York.

Robert C. Hayden
Boston, Massachusetts
1992

THE FORERUNNERS

Onesimus was an enslaved person who contributed to progress in medicine during America's colonial period. His knowledge led to the use of inoculation in the Boston, Massachusetts, area as a way to prevent people from catching smallpox.

In 1721, Onesimus was "the property" of Cotton Mather. When Mather asked Onesimus if he had ever had smallpox, he answered, "Yes and no." What did Onesimus mean by "Yes and no"?

Onesimus described a procedure that he had undergone in Africa. On his arm was a scar where he had been cut with a sharp knife. A bit of pus from the sore of a person who had a bad smallpox infection had been placed in the cut. The pus contained the smallpox germ, and once in Onesimus' body, it had given him a very mild case of smallpox. This practice produced a mild case of smallpox on purpose, making the body immune to a more severe attack in the future.

Mather thought that the African method of inoculation should be tried in America. He contacted 10 doctors in Boston and told them about the practice of deliberately infecting healthy persons with smallpox to keep them from catching the disease accidentally.

One of the doctors, a Dr. Boylston, tried the inoculation on his own son and two of his enslaved Africans. It worked. Later, Dr. Boylston inoculated 241 people, and only six caught smallpox.

Although other doctors used the method described by Onesimus, there was strong opposition to the practice of inoculation. Some religious leaders charged that it was a non-Christian or heathen practice. Angry mobs attacked the homes of Mather and Boylston. When a few patients died after smallpox inoculations, even more people became fearful of the technique. Some doctors claimed that the number of deaths from inoculations was as great as from the disease itself.

In the 1790s, the British doctor Edward Jenner perfected an inoculation technique using a less dangerous kind of smallpox germ. Today, the smallpox vaccination has conquered the spread of this dreaded disease.

During the American Revolutionary War, the African method of inoculation against smallpox was used to prevent soldiers from getting the disease. Because Onesimus passed the idea on to Dr. Boylston, the ravages of smallpox were lessened.

This is one example of the contributions of African Americans to medical science. African-American men and women have been demonstrating their interest and ability in the field of medicine for a long time.

As early as 1667, an African by the name of Lucas Santomée Peters was trained in medicine in Holland. He practiced in the colony of New York under the Dutch and the British. When the British took over New York, the governor gave him land in return for medical services.

In early New England, slaves who served doctors often served as medical apprentices to their masters. In time, some of these apprentices became doctors on their own. One of them, Primus, enslaved in Connecticut, helped his owner in surgery and in the general practice of medicine. When the doctor died, Primus took over his master's practice. He was reported as being "extraordinarily successful throughout the county." His master's white patients did not mind being treated by him.

Papan, enslaved in Virginia, also learned medicine from his master. Papan's treatment of skin and venereal diseases was extremely effective. His work in medicine was so outstanding that the Virginia legislature bought him from his master in 1729 and set him free from slavery to practice medicine for the benefit of the people of Virginia. In 1733, another enslaved Virginian, one who had discovered cures for scurvy and distemper, was also freed by the state and given a pension for life.

Many Africans brought to America proven methods of relieving pain and treating diseases. The control of disease by using the roots of plants and various herbs was widely practiced on the African continent long before the discovery of America. In Africa, the medical value of minerals and plant substances had been learned through practical experience. When Africans found themselves in America, it was only natural that they would continue using their proven methods of treatment.

Many enslaved people gained such wide reputations for their healing powers within the slave community that they attracted the attention of whites.

As early as 1792, a slave named Cesar had gained a reputation for his use of roots and herbs to cure poisoning. Cesar's remedy for a rattlesnake bite was published in *The Massachusetts Magazine*. The state of North Carolina purchased his freedom and gave him a pension of $500 a year for life.

The first African American to be widely recognized as a doctor was James Derham. Born in 1762 in Philadelphia, he was a slave to Dr. John Kearsley, Jr., one of the most noted doctors of his time. Though slaves were not supposed to be taught to read or write, the family who owned Derham gave him instruction.

James Derham took an early interest in the medical profession of his master. When Derham was a teen-ager, Dr. Kearsley allowed him to mix medicines and give them to his patients. After Dr. Kearsley's death, Derham was sold to a Dr. West, a surgeon in the British army during the Revolutionary War. During the war, Derham served Dr. West in some of the duties of caring for injured soldiers.

At the end of the war, Derham was sold to Dr. Robert Dove of New Orleans, who used him as an assistant. After several years, Dr. Dove gave his assistant his freedom in recognition of the outstanding work he had done. Derham was able to practice medicine on his own and earned as much as $3,000 a year—a very large income at the time. In 1788, at 26 years of age, James Derham was regarded as one of the most eminent doctors in New Orleans.

The most noted African-American doctor after James Derham was Dr. James McCune Smith. A graduate of the University of Glasgow in Scotland, Smith began to practice medicine in New York about 1837. He soon distinguished himself as a skilled physician and surgeon and served on the staffs of hospitals with a number of white doctors.

Dr. Smith lived during a time when science was being used to try to prove the inferiority of black people. He attacked this argument with a strong speech on "The Comparative Anatomy of the Races." In Chapter 4, you will read about Dr. William Montague Cobb, another African-American physician who, through his research and writing on anatomy, fought the same myth of racial inferiority nearly a hundred years later.

The next African-American physician of prominence was Martin R. Delany. Born in 1812 in Charleston, West Virginia, he was a free black who grew up in Pennsylvania. Delany began to study medicine when he was 19 years old as an apprentice in Pittsburgh. He abandoned medicine for a while to fight the Fugitive Slave Law of 1850.

Delany worked for the anti-slavery cause and helped freed slaves who wished to return to Africa. He returned to Pittsburgh in 1851 to continue his medical studies near Doctors Joseph P. Gazzen and Francis J. Lemoyne. After being refused admission to the University of Pennsylvania and medical schools in New York because he was a black man, Delany was finally admitted to the medical school of Harvard University.

After he left Harvard, Dr. Delany, like Dr. Smith before him, became involved in the argument over the superiority and inferiority of the races. Delany traveled throughout the country using his medical knowledge to defend the intelligence and ability of African Americans.

Dr. Delany returned to Pittsburgh to practice. He was a leader in treating cholera during the epidemic of 1854. His worth to the community was shown when he was appointed to a city board that gave medical advice to poor people, both black and white. During the Civil War, Dr. Delany served in the infantry as a major in the U.S. Army.

Like many black doctors, Delany devoted most of his free time to improving conditions for his people. When not practicing medicine, he was traveling at home and abroad speaking out against slavery. In Ohio, Delany was beaten, almost fatally, by a mob of whites when he spoke for the freedom of those held in bondage.

One of the first accounts of dentistry among African Americans appeared in the *Pennsylvania Gazette* in 1740. It was reported that a black man named Simon was able to "bleed and draw teeth" and "was a great doctor among his people." Another early African-American dentist was a Dr. Zeke, who practiced in both Savannah and Augusta, Georgia, where he offered his services to whites in the daytime and to blacks at night.

Robert and Roderick Badger were pioneer dentists in the 1800s. Robert Badger was born in 1829, his brother, Roderick, in 1834, in DeKalb County, Georgia. They were sons of a white dentist and a black woman who was one of his slaves. The Badger brothers learned dentistry from their master-father.

Robert Badger was a rural dentist who earned his living traveling on horseback from county to county around Atlanta, Georgia. His brother, Roderick, arrived in Atlanta, Georgia, in 1856 to start a practice. Both the Badger brothers faced great prejudice from whites as they tried to practice their profession.

In May 1859, a petition was presented to the Atlanta city council in opposition to Roderick Badger. Part of it read as follows:

> We feel aggrieved, as Southern citizens, that your honorable body tolerates a Negro dentist (Roderick Badger) in our midst, and in justice to ourselves and the community, it ought to be abated. We, the residents of Atlanta, appeal to you for justice.

Despite this kind of opposition, the Badger brothers continued with their profession. And both became leading citizens of Atlanta.

The first African American to receive an education in dentistry and a dental degree from an American medical school was Robert Tanner Freeman. Born in 1847 to slave parents in North Carolina, he was among the first six graduates in dental medicine from Harvard University in 1867. After graduating from Harvard, Freeman practiced dentistry for many years in Washington, D.C.

Another early graduate of the Harvard Dental School was George F. Grant. He finished dental school in 1870 and was the school's first African-American instructor, serving for many years as a demonstrator of Mechanical Dentistry and as an instructor in the treatment of a condition known as cleft palate.

Grant's invention of a device to correct cleft palate brought him national recognition. He also operated a large and successful practice in Boston which consisted mostly of white patients. He was known for his skill in making and fitting false teeth.

These sketches of some African-American doctors of the eighteenth and nineteenth centuries only begin to tell the story. To show the depth and richness of the lives and contributions of African Americans to medicine, eleven doctors are described in the following chapters.

All the doctors in this book are twentieth-century Americans. Four of them are still living. Each has lived a unique and meaningful life. And each has done something to raise the health standards of the country through medical practice, research, or teaching.

But each of these black men and women has been more than a doctor—more than a fighter of disease in a laboratory or hospital, more than a healer of human illness, more than a medical teacher. Each has had to face and conquer a "disease" left over from the days of the American slavery of black people—the disease of prejudice and discrimination against those of African ancestry.

Each of these doctors has met race discrimination in a different way. Their lives show us what it has meant to be both a doctor of medicine and an African American.

SOLOMON CARTER FULLER

1

John Lewis Fuller was a slave in Petersburg, Virginia, during the late 1700s. He was a skilled bootmaker and shoemaker for his white master. With some of the money that his master allowed him to keep, Fuller was able to buy his freedom. He was also able to buy his wife's freedom from slavery.

By the late 1700s, quite a few African slaves in the United States had bought their freedom. Other slaves had gained their freedom because they fought in the American Revolutionary War.

These free black people—educated, highly skilled in crafts and business, and fairly prosperous—were unhappy with their lowly place in American life. Because they were outspoken *against* slavery and *for* the civil rights of African Americans, both enslaved and free, they were seen as a source of trouble for slave owners. There was heated discussion in white America about what to do with these free and discontented blacks.

One answer was to return the former slaves to Africa. Some African Americans organized themselves and raised money to send ex-slaves back to Africa, where they or their parents had been born.

A group of whites founded the American Colonization Society to set up a colony of emigrant blacks in Africa. In 1816, the West African republic of Liberia was officially established as a home for former slaves. To this end, the U.S. Congress created the American Society for Colonizing Free People of Color. It was argued by many that "the sons of Africa" should, in justice, be returned to "the land of their fathers."

In 1822, a settlement at the site of Monrovia, the capital city of Liberia, was the beginning of a new life for a few thousand former slaves. John Lewis Fuller was one of the former slaves who left America with help from the American Colonization Society during the early 1800s.

About 60 years later, during the summer of 1889, a boat left the shores of Liberia's west coast on its way to America. One of its passengers was the grandson of John Lewis Fuller. Solomon C. Fuller was 17 years old when he left his homeland, headed for the southern United States, where his grandfather had been a slave.

Solomon Fuller was traveling to America to further his education, and he went on to become a pioneering medical doctor in the diagnosis and treatment of mental illness (psychiatry) and diseases of the nervous system (neuropathology).

Between 1899 and 1933, the year of his retirement, Dr. Fuller gained national and international respect and recognition for his research and teaching as well as for his treatment of mental illness.

Today, Solomon Fuller's portrait hangs in the offices of the American Psychiatric Association in Washington, D.C., along with those of other great figures in the history of American psychiatry.

From Africa to America

Solomon Carter Fuller was born in Monrovia, Liberia, in 1872. His father, also named Solomon Carter Fuller, was a coffee planter and a Liberian government official. His mother, Anna Ursala James, was the daughter of Mr. and Mrs. Benjamin Van Ranseler James, both doctors and church missionaries from the United States. Solomon and his brother, Thomas, were educated at the school their parents had established on the coffee plantation.

In September 1889, Fuller arrived in Salisbury, North Carolina, to attend Livingston College. Livingston was a college for black students. Fuller was the only student in his class from Africa.

By 1893, Solomon Fuller had achieved his first goal—graduation from college with his bachelor's degree. From Livingston, he moved north to begin medical studies at Long Island College Hospital in Brooklyn, New York.

But Fuller spent only a year there before he moved to Boston, Massachusetts, to continue his training at the Boston University School of Medicine. Fuller accomplished his second goal in 1897, when he was awarded his medical degree. He could now be called "Doctor" Fuller.

Dr. Fuller was pleased with his college opportunities and achievement in America. At the same time, he was also disillusioned by the racial discrimination that he and other black people faced. Fuller's African background—shaped by his mother's church work—had been extremely religious, and he was so deeply shocked and disturbed by the alienation between the races that he didn't attend or participate in church or religious affairs in this country.

"All during my teen years I tried to get Dad to come back to the church," said his son Solomon C. Fuller, Jr., "but I didn't succeed."

Though bitter about the disrespect shown to African Americans, Dr. Fuller kept busy with his medical practice and research, hoping to help bring about a change in white America's racial views through his work in medicine. Unlike his grandfather, Solomon Fuller chose not to return to Liberia, but to remain in America and to try to create a better life for himself and others.

Upon his graduation from medical school, Dr. Fuller received an internship at Westborough State Hospital for the Insane in Massachusetts. There, he began his career in the research of brain diseases.

And there, too, Solomon Fuller met his future wife, Meta Vaux Warrick, who became one of America's most noted artists.

Searching for the Causes

At Westborough, Solomon Fuller began to examine cells and tissues from the brains of deceased people who had suffered from mental illness. He looked for changes in brain matter that might explain certain types of abnormal human behavior and death caused by nerve diseases.

In Fuller's laboratory was an instrument that could slice brain tissue into segments so thin that light could pass through the slices. Since light could pass through these thin sections, Dr. Fuller was able to take pictures, or photomicrographs, of the brain cells.

Solomon Fuller was known for his work on different forms of mental illness (psychosis). A person who suffers from a psychosis may lose thinking and reasoning powers and may exhibit behavior that is dangerous to that person or other people. Dr. Fuller sought to find a relationship between a patient's thinking and behavior patterns and any changes in brain cells that could be detected in the photomicrographs.

Solomon Fuller also worked on a form of mental disease known as Alzheimer's disease. Named for the doctor who first observed the condition in humans, this disease, associated with aging, results in memory loss, impaired thinking, and disorientation.

The work that Dr. Fuller carried out at Westborough State Hospital on degenerative diseases of the brain was widely recognized by other psychiatrists. In 1909, he was invited to take part in a landmark conference at Clark University in Worcester, Massachusetts. The event marked Sigmund Freud's first visit to the United States, and a photo taken at the meeting shows Dr. Fuller with Freud, Carl Jung, and Alfred Adler, the leading figures in the development of modern psychiatry.

Dr. Fuller lived at Westborough State Hospital during his early years there. He was immersed in medical practice and research and spent long hours each day at his work. His only relaxation was fishing in a pond at the back of the hospital.

In 1911, Solomon Fuller reported the ninth known case of Alzheimer's disease. Fuller suggested that something other than hardening of the arteries, then a common explanation for the disorder, was the actual cause of the disease. More than 40 years later, in 1953—the year of Dr. Fuller's death—two other medical researchers confirmed his findings.

The cause of Alzheimer's is still unknown, and no cure has been found. Some 2.6 million elderly people have the disease today. And it is estimated that by the year

2000 more than 4 million people will have the disorder. (Alzheimer's was not a major public health concern in the early 1900s because so few people lived beyond age 75. In contrast, more than 50 percent of the U.S. population now reaches age 75; 25 percent of the population lives to age 85. Therefore, the incidence of Alzheimer's is much higher today than it was in Dr. Fuller's time.)

A Full Life

Meta Vaux Warrick, an artist from Philadelphia, met Dr. Fuller while she was paying a visit to Westborough State College. Warrick had been studying art, particularly sculpture, in Philadelphia and Paris. When she learned about Dr. Fuller's knowledge of medical photography, she suggested that he might enjoy portrait photography.

Her suggestion began a lifelong hobby for Solomon Fuller. He became a skilled experimenter in photographing old portrait prints.

After Solomon Fuller and Meta Warrick were married in 1909, the couple moved into a new home in Framingham, Massachusetts, not far from Dr. Fuller's laboratory at Westborough. There, Fuller opened an office for private practice, worked at his photography, and engaged in book-binding and gardening. There, he and Meta raised their three sons.

Solomon Fuller's work at Westborough continued long after his internship. In 1899, just two years after arriving at Westborough, Fuller was appointed the hospital's head pathologist. It was in that year that Dr. Fuller began a

45-year career at the Westborough hospital, serving 22 years as a pathologist and 23 years as a consultant in diseases of the nervous system.

Fuller expanded the work of the hospital laboratory and added to its staff. In 1913, he became the editor of the *Westborough State Hospital Papers*, a journal reporting the current medical research of doctors on the hospital's staff. Dr. Fuller's own writings appeared in this journal as well as in medical textbooks and scientific journals around the country.

In 1899, the same year that Fuller was named head pathologist at Westborough, he received an appointment to teach at the Boston University School of Medicine, the school from which he had graduated only two years earlier. Between 1899 and 1933, when he retired from Boston University, Fuller was an instructor and lecturer on the causes and treatment of nervous system diseases. As an authority in the field of mental disorders, Solomon Fuller gave to Boston University more than 30 years of devoted teaching and research.

Pride and Prejudice

Solomon Fuller was proud of his African ancestry and proud to be a black American. But he was disturbed to find himself thought of as an excellent "colored doctor." Fuller didn't want to be known as a "colored" psychiatrist. Rather, he felt that his medical achievements should be evaluated on their merit alone.

This bitterness Fuller kept to himself, however.

Although he was a very popular and highly respected teacher and researcher as well as a recognized authority in psychiatry, Dr. Fuller faced racial discrimination. He was never officially placed on the payroll at Boston University School of Medicine, although he did draw a small salary for his teaching there.

During his last five years at Boston University, Fuller served as head of the Department of Neurology, but he was never given the title to go with the responsibilities. Eventually, a white assistant professor was made a full professor—a title that Solomon Fuller was never given— and was appointed head of the department.

In his later years, Fuller became somewhat resentful at not receiving the titles to go with the teaching positions that he held. His resentment was provoked in part by friends and associates who felt that he was being treated unfairly because of his race. At one time, he was receiving $24 a month while others received $28 for doing the same job. But he took pride in his work and accepted less than his due with a gracefulness that was uniquely his.

The Man and His Books

A typical day for Dr. Solomon Fuller was long and full. It started around 9:30 in the morning and often didn't end until long after midnight.

The mornings were spent at the Westborough Hospital laboratory while afternoons were devoted to teaching in Boston at the medical school. But his day did not end with his teaching.

When he arrived home in Framingham in the late afternoon, there would be patients waiting to see him. They would sometimes come as late as nine or ten o'clock in the evening. His day wasn't over when the last patient left, either—there was still reading to be done, for both his medical work and pleasure.

Dr. Fuller was an avid reader, often reading until two o'clock in the morning. He was a great collector of books. There weren't many that he couldn't read in a single sitting. Bookbinding was another one of his hobbies, along with photography.

"He seemed to spend everything he had on books," recalled his son Solomon, Jr. Dr. Fuller was fond of picking up old books in dilapidated condition from secondhand bookstores and converting them into beautifully bound collectors' items.

Fuller learned all phases of the bookbinding craft. He even tooled and decorated his own leather for covering old books. He bought old prints, too, which he photographed and gave to his friends.

Continuing Education

Research and teaching were only two of the ways in which Solomon Fuller contributed to his field. As a young psychiatrist, he went wherever there was something to be learned, wherever there was someone doing research that would give him new knowledge or some person who could give him new ideas. He traveled and studied in Europe and at various medical institutions in this country.

In 1904, Solomon Fuller went to Germany to study at the Psychiatric Clinic of the University of Munich as well as the Pathological Institute of the same university. In Europe, he studied with medical researchers who were developing a new approach to medicine—the biochemical or physical causes of disease. One of those researchers he studied with in Germany was Dr. Alois Alzheimer.

One of the most exciting moments in Dr. Fuller's life occurred one afternoon on a sightseeing visit in Berlin, Germany. He was passing by the house of the Nobel Prize winner Paul Ehrlich, and on an impulse he knocked on Ehrlich's front door just to say hello. Ehrlich had received the Nobel Prize in 1908 for his work in immunology. He was a man whom Dr. Fuller had long admired for his scientific research. But Solomon Fuller was a complete stranger to Ehrlich.

To his surprise, Dr. Fuller found that Ehrlich lived alone and was eager for someone to talk with. Dr. Fuller ended up spending the entire afternoon with the famous German scientist.

This chance meeting led to a lifelong friendship. Dr. Fuller later told his sons and others that the afternoon with Ehrlich was one of the most profitable events and lasting memories of his life. He had not been content just to stand on that Berlin street in 1905. He had reached out to meet a person he had long admired. The experience, Fuller claimed, enriched the rest of his life.

Before returning from Europe, Dr. Fuller made his only trip back to Liberia to visit his mother and brother.

He resumed work in the United States with new ideas and skills acquired in Europe.

A New Way of Looking at Things

Fuller began to look at mental illness in a different way. His work centered on physical, or organic, changes in the body that cause different forms of mental disorder. His focus on the organic causes of mental disorder led him into research on schizophrenia, mental illness connected with old age, disorders connected with alcoholism, and inherited brain diseases.

Dr. Fuller was also interested in behavioral or mental problems that appeared to have no organic causes. Some people suffered from mental illness because of maladjustment to daily living. Fuller began to explore the effects of life experiences on a person's thinking and behavior. He began to study and practice psychotherapy. This form of therapy treats a patient's problems through counseling and discussion, helping the patient to analyze his or her own behavior and feelings.

His studies in Europe helped Fuller to build bridges in his medical specialty. He learned that there was more to mental illness than understanding the changes and deterioration of brain cells. Dr. Fuller's medical interests began to shift from neuropsychiatry to psychotherapy. A neuropsychiatrist looks for and studies changes in the structure and chemicals of nerve cells in the brain, the kinds of changes that might cause problems or differences in a person's behavior. A psychotherapist looks for and treats abnormal behavior that appears not to be caused by any physical change in nerve cells or tissue.

Dr. Fuller helped to bring the European frontiers of psychiatric research and knowledge to the United States. He was a leading pioneer of new approaches for diagnosing and treating brain disease and abnormal human behavior. Fuller's writings in medical books and journals (and his work as a member of the American Psychiatric Association, the Boston Society for Psychiatry and Neurology, the New York Psychiatric Association, the Massachusetts Medical Society, the New England Medical Society, and the American Medical Association) influenced the thinking and practice of other doctors in the field of mental health.

Encouraging other African-American doctors was one of Solomon Fuller's strong interests and contributions to medicine. In 1923, he trained four black medical-school graduates in neuropsychiatry. These students went on to serve at the Tuskegee Veterans Administration Hospital in Tuskegee, Alabama, a hospital serving hundreds of black people in the segregated South.

Some of the students Dr. Fuller guided went on to prominent careers in medicine. Dr. George Branch became chief of Psychiatric Service of the Veterans Administration Hospital at Tuskegee. Dr. Charles Pinderhughes became a professor of psychiatry at Boston University and the coordinator of residency training at Bedford (Massachusetts) Veterans Administration Hospital.

"Though growing old, Dr. Fuller still acted like an eager, young medical student as he talked with me about the newest ideas and methods of treating mental illness," recalled Dr. Pinderhughes.

Dr. Pinderhughes continued:

> Talking with Dr. Fuller was a great education for me because he had worked and studied with the great minds in twentieth-century psychiatry and psychoanalysis. In an era when the professional development of black people was discouraged and inadequately rewarded, Dr. Fuller persevered until he secured the finest training available. And what he knew helped me.

Counselor and Friend

Dr. Fuller's private psychiatric practice was a large one. All kinds of people came to him for counseling and treatment—rich and poor, both black and white. Fuller also worked with the Framingham Police Department, examining criminals who showed dangerous behavior and appearing in court to report on a criminal's mental health.

Patients often traveled long distances to be with Dr. Fuller for psychotherapy. He always took plenty of time with each patient. "My father had great spiritual qualities," remarked his son Solomon, Jr.

His son continued: "People came to him for a spiritual communion that was a refreshing, inspiring, and motivating experience. Some people kept coming back to him right up until the time of his death—not for treatment of a mental disorder, but just to have a spiritual exchange with him. My father had such a gracious, loving, radiant, and quieting personality that it had a great calming effect on his patients' problems."

One of the doctors who often visited Dr. Fuller was Dr. William Hinton, the subject of Chapter 2 in this book. Dr. Fuller counseled his friend and colleague privately. Dr. Hinton (with his wife and two daughters) and Dr. Fuller (with his wife and three sons) would take turns visiting each other's homes.

The two doctors would talk about medical research, their students, and the problems that they faced each day. But that was not all they talked about, for they had a hobby in common.

They shared a love of gardening.

Dr. Fuller, like Dr. Hinton, was a master gardener and a lover of plants. The two men were always comparing their gardens, and there was a certain rivalry between them as to who had the most healthy and beautiful plants. Dr. Fuller took great pride in transplanting and cultivating his favorites.

While Dr. Fuller worked in his garden, Meta Fuller worked in her art studio. Throughout her life, she pursued her interest in sculpture. Meta Fuller achieved recognition as one of America's outstanding African-American artists. Today, her work can be found at the New York Public Library, Howard University (in Washington, D.C.), and at various art museums throughout the country. A bronze bust of Dr. Fuller done by his wife stands in the lobby of the Solomon Carter Fuller Mental Health Center in Boston, Massachusetts.

Dr. Fuller retired from Boston University in 1933. The last 20 years of his life were somewhat tragic.

The Final Years

In the mid-1930s, Solomon Fuller, who suffered from diabetes, became thin and frail. In 1944, he began to lose his eyesight. But he was not willing to give up his practice, and he continued to treat patients until the time of his death. Dr. Pinderhughes traveled to Framingham to help Dr. Fuller continue his practice when he could no longer see. "I would give his patients the physical examination, and Dr. Fuller, blind and aged, would do the rest," recalls Dr. Pinderhughes.

Without sight, Dr. Fuller would kneel in his backyard garden, tending his plants and planting new seedlings. He could not see the weeds, though, so they grew freely and finally overran his garden.

Blindness robbed Dr. Fuller of his favorite pleasure—reading. He had to be content with having his sons and friends read to him. The radio was also used to take the place of books now that he could no longer read.

At Christmas, two years before his death, he gave his son Thomas a book on fishing. *The Complete Angler, or The Contemplative Man's Recreation, Being a Discourse of Rivers, Fish Ponds, Fish and Fishing*, written in 1887, was one of the first books that Dr. Fuller had rebound and covered with leather.

Dr. Fuller was open to questioning and would sit for long periods of time talking about the past. Pulling on his pointed white beard, he recalled stories from his early life in Liberia and the great people he had met through his work in medicine, doctors such as Sigmund Freud and civil rights leaders such as William E. B. Du Bois.

Dr. Fuller lived a full and useful life to the end. A friend who visited the doctor shortly before Fuller's death in 1953 wrote the following description of him:

> I saw him and talked with him; though blind, his memory was excellent, his speech flawless, his interest alive. He knew he had not long to live, but accepted the fact in his unusual philosophical manner, like the perfect gentleman he was.

WILLIAM A. HINTON

2

William "Gus" Hinton was awarded his Doctor of Medicine degree in 1912 from Harvard Medical School, but he couldn't treat a sick person in a Boston, Massachusetts, hospital. At the time of William Hinton's graduation, black doctors were not allowed to practice in any of Boston's hospitals. It wasn't until 1931 that the first black doctor was admitted to an internship at Boston City Hospital.

As a young medical-school graduate, William Hinton had wanted to be a surgeon. He later wrote, "My ambition . . . was to prepare myself to practice and teach surgery in the South, particularly among an underprivileged group which was in need of medical services. But this ambition wasn't realized."

Hinton was unable to get an internship in a Boston hospital because of his race. (The reason given was that married men were not admitted as interns.) But he was not discouraged from pursuing a career in medicine. He turned instead to laboratory work.

Fifteen years after graduating from medical school, Dr. Hinton had developed an important blood test for the dreaded disease of syphilis. The Hinton Test, as it became widely known, was used throughout the country for the next 25 years.

In 1935, the Hinton Test was adopted as the official laboratory test for syphilis at the Massachusetts Department of Public Health and at all hospitals in the state. Few people knew that it had been developed by a black man. In 1936, Hinton's book, *Syphilis and Its Treatment,* became the first medical textbook written by an African American to be published.

Syphilis is a social disease. It is caused by a germ that can be passed from one person to another through sexual contact. Once in the blood stream, the syphilis germs multiply and begin to attack the nerve cells. This disease can affect boys and girls, men and women, and people of all ages, races, and classes.

Although syphilis is not as widespread today as it was 60 years ago, it is still one of the most dangerous and crippling diseases known. It can cause sterility, blindness, and even death. Teen-agers and young adults who are sexually active are particularly susceptible to syphilis.

William Hinton devoted his entire professional life—a period of more than 30 years—to fighting this disease. He was respected throughout the country as an authority in the field of social diseases. When Hinton retired as director of the Department of Clinical Laboratories at the Boston Dispensary in 1952, Christian Herter, then governor of Massachusetts, wrote in a letter of tribute, "Your name is known the world over for singular achievements which have benefited all of mankind."

An Education in Values

William Hinton was born in Chicago, Illinois, in 1883. His parents, Maria and Augustus Hinton, who had been slaves in North Carolina, had moved to Chicago after being freed at the end of the Civil War.

Shortly after the birth of their son, the Hintons moved to Kansas City, Kansas, where William Hinton grew up. His parents were determined to give him the advantages of an education that they had not enjoyed. While attending Kansas City public schools and a private Catholic school, young William earned money as a newsboy, raised chickens, and did odd jobs to help his family.

Hinton's parents shaped their son's values. "Although born in slavery and without formal education, they recognized and practiced not only the highest ideals in their personal conduct," William Hinton wrote, "but also the true democratic principle of equal opportunity for all, without regard to racial or religious origins or to economic or political status."

By the time he was 16, Hinton had completed his high-school studies. An interest in medicine was sparked by his biology teacher. He attended the University of Kansas in 1900, but in 1902 Hinton had to drop out of college for lack of money. He worked for a year to earn money so that he could return to college.

During the year that Hinton was away, the University of Kansas changed its program of studies. In 1903, therefore, Hinton transferred to Harvard College in Cambridge, Massachusetts, where he graduated in 1905, determined on a career in medicine. Lacking money, Hinton could not enter medical school right away.

William Hinton spent the next four years teaching biology, chemistry, and physics at colleges in Tennessee and Oklahoma. He also taught embryology at Meharry Medical College. At the Agricultural and Mechanical College in Langston, Oklahoma, he met Ada Hawes, also a young teacher, who became Hinton's wife and a strong supporter of his work in medicine.

Throughout his teaching years, William Hinton never lost sight of his goal of becoming a doctor. During the summers, he continued his instruction in medicine by studying bacteriology and physiology at the University of Chicago. He was always preparing himself for the future.

In 1909, William Hinton was back in Boston as a member of the first-year class of Harvard Medical School.

Despite his four-year absence from full-time study, Hinton moved through medical school quickly—and with high grades. He won the Wigglesworth Scholarship two years in a row. He refused to accept the Hayden Scholarship, established for black students, because he wanted to be rewarded on his merit, not compensated because of his race.

Hinton supported himself and his wife by assisting Dr. Richard C. Cabot and Dr. Elmer E. Southard. Both were outstanding instructors, and both were sources of inspiration to Hinton. Dr. Southard was so impressed by his student's knowledge of syphilis that he arranged for Hinton to begin teaching at Harvard Medical School about the laboratory detection of the disease.

William Hinton's life in medical school was not free from racial discrimination. Medical students received bedside instruction at Boston Lying-In Hospital. Hinton and his instructors were concerned that he, being black, would not be accepted by the patients. As it turned out, however, his presence was accepted by most patients, but some fellow medical students who had been assigned to work with him refused to do so.

In 1912, after only three years of study, Dr. Hinton graduated with honors from Harvard Medical School. It usually took four years to complete the work that he had accomplished in three, but despite his successful record as a medical student, Hinton's future was uncertain. All medical-school graduates had to go through a period of training, or an internship, in a hospital. Boston hospitals would not accept black doctors as interns, however.

"But for Hinton's courage, determination, and perseverance, his contributions to humanity might have been lost," observed Dr. Cabot about his former student. "He was determined to succeed without benefit of an internship which is considered essential for every doctor."

In 1912, William Hinton began working each morning as a volunteer assistant in the Department of Pathology of Massachusetts General Hospital. In the afternoons, he worked as a paid assistant in the Wassermann Laboratory of the Harvard Medical School. Unable to treat patients in Boston hospitals, he turned to studying the blood serum from some of these patients.

At the Wassermann Laboratory, blood samples were studied to detect and diagnose certain diseases, including syphilis. The laboratory, a state laboratory based at Harvard Medical School, was named for the man who devised the first test for syphilis in 1906.

The weaknesses and limitations of the Wassermann Test were obvious. The test sometimes showed positive results when the patient wasn't infected with the syphilis germ (a "false positive"). Doctors were beginning to lose confidence in the reliability of the Wassermann Test.

Dr. Hinton began working to design a better test.

In 1915, the Wassermann Laboratory was transferred from Harvard University to the Massachusetts Department of Public Health. Dr. Hinton was appointed director of the laboratory, a position he held for 38 years. For the next 12 years, he immersed himself in investigating a new and better test for syphilis.

In 1916, a young high-school graduate by the name of Genevieve Stuart was appointed to the Wassermann Laboratory as a secretary to Dr. Hinton. For the remainder of her professional life, she worked closely beside this doctor who was to obtain national and international fame.

After two years of typing, filing, answering the phones, and keeping records for Dr. Hinton, Stuart began to learn lab techniques from him. She started by performing blood tests for syphilis and went on to master other laboratory procedures. She remained Dr. Hinton's assistant for nearly 40 years.

When interviewed at the age of 78, Stuart remembered the early days in Dr. Hinton's lab:

> When I went into the laboratory end of it, he was a very patient teacher. He taught most of the people who came to work at the laboratory. We were doing 100 Wassermann Tests a day and also diagnosing animal heads for rabies. If you didn't have brains according to him, he just didn't want you in the lab. Dr. Hinton was very fussy about how things were done. He was a perfectionist.

The Hinton Test and the Hinton Garden

There were really only two worlds in Dr. Hinton's life after 1915. His laboratory was one. The other world was Hinton's home in Canton, Massachusetts, about 20 miles south of Boston. The Hintons had lived in Cambridge since Dr. Hinton's medical-school days, but their house was too small. In 1916, they bought a house on four acres of land in Canton. They had not seen the inside of the house before they bought it. "The house isn't worth anything," the owner had told them. "What you're getting is the land."

When the Hintons took over, the tiny house was in shambles. The walls were covered with bugs. The house was more like a shack than anything else, but the Hintons had dreams for their newly acquired home and land.

On weekends and during each vacation, repairs and improvements were made. Several rooms and a porch were added. The tool shed, barn, and garage each represented a vacation's work. Flowers, fruit trees, and a lily pond surrounded the home after a few years. The Hintons had rebuilt the place with their own hands. "I'm really just as concerned about the Japanese beetles and other bugs that eat my roses as I am about those that I find under my laboratory microscope," Dr. Hinton once observed.

When William Hinton wasn't working on his home, he was working at his laboratory. In addition to heading the Wassermann Laboratory, Hinton was also the director of the Laboratory Department of the Boston Dispensary, a position he had also assumed in 1915. He spent his mornings at the dispensary and afternoons at the Wassermann Laboratory. Saturdays were not a part of the weekend, but full workdays for Dr. Hinton and his staff.

In 1919, Hinton received an appointment as instructor in Preventive Medicine and Hygiene at the Harvard Medical School. That appointment marked the beginning of a 34-year teaching career at Harvard.

William Hinton proved to be not only an outstanding researcher and laboratory director, but also an inspiring instructor. "The students all loved him," his lab assistant recalled. His manner of teaching was easy and informal—friendly, humorous, and appealing. Hinton's lectures often ended with spontaneous applause by the students.

In 1931, William Hinton's interest in training people for careers in medicine was still strong. At the Boston Dispensary, Hinton started a school for training women to become laboratory technicians. These classes grew into one of the country's leading schools for preparing medical technicians. Hinton's graduates were hired by hospitals and laboratories throughout the country.

The Hinton program was one of the first to help meet the growing demand for technicians well versed in new laboratory techniques. The program survives today as part of a medical training program at Northeastern University in Boston. Hinton encouraged women to become medical technicians at a time when they were not readily accepted in the medical world.

Meanwhile, Hinton continued to carry on his research in the pathology of venereal diseases. Blood serum, test tubes, cultures, and chemicals—these occupied more and more of Hinton's time. Lunch hours were spent in the laboratory. "All I ever saw him with was a cup of coffee," noted his assistant.

While continuing his research, Hinton was responsible for the syphilis testing being done in Massachusetts. In addition, he had taken over the rabies work for the

State Division of Animal Husbandry. When the state began requiring blood tests of couples before marriage and of mothers before the birth of babies, Dr. Hinton supervised the expansion of the state laboratory facilities. At the time of his appointment, there were 10 state laboratories. He increased the number to 117. Hinton's laboratory was also conducting research on tuberculosis and influenza.

Dr. Hinton's most important contribution to medicine, however, was his work with syphilis. Only two years after his medical-school graduation, Hinton had published his first scientific paper on the disease. His understanding of syphilis was so comprehensive that William Hinton was asked to write the chapter on syphilis for the *Textbook of Preventive Medicine.*

By 1927, Hinton had perfected his blood serum test for syphilis. After 12 years of painstaking laboratory work, the Hinton Test was rated outstanding because of both its sensitivity and specificity.

Hinton's method drastically reduced the large number of "false positive" results that were given by the Wassermann method. Because the treatment of syphilis at that time was painful and dangerous and because the stigma of venereal disease was so dreaded, an accurate test was of utmost importance.

In the Hinton Test, a sample of the liquid portion of a patient's blood, called serum, was combined in a test tube with a mixture of glycerin solution, sodium chloride, and a substance that was prepared from powdered beef heart muscle. The tube was shaken vigorously for three minutes to mix the serum with the other substances and then placed overnight in a warm water bath. In the morning, the tube was held up to a bright light and examined for a whitish ring of particles at the top of the fluid. If the coarse particles appeared, the syphilis test was positive; the patient was carrying the syphilis germ. If there were no white particles, the test was negative; the patient was not syphilitic.

Dr. Hinton's test was 98 percent accurate. It was the most sensitive and accurate test ever designed to diagnose syphilis. But Hinton wasn't completely satisfied, and he worked for four more years to perfect his technique.

By 1931, William Hinton had developed an improved test which could be done with smaller amounts of blood. Dr. John Davies had worked along with Hinton in the modification of the test, and it became known as the Hinton-Davies Test. It was adopted as the official test of the Massachusetts Department of Public Health in its state lab in 1935. Outside of Massachusetts, the test became widely known and was used for more than 20 years.

Scientist and Author

While his lab commanded much of his time, Hinton could still escape to Canton. On many a summer day, his laboratory would be decorated with flowers from his garden. His staff and colleagues at the medical school enjoyed the vegetables grown by Hinton and his wife. Ada Hinton also loved to garden. She constantly had her hands and knees in the soil.

The Hintons made sure that their orchard and gardens had every possible variety of plant that would grow in New England.

Corn, beans, and tomatoes were grown each summer. One day, Dr. Hinton had picked some beans to share with the doctors at the medical school. But his wife, Ada, was quick to object. "I raised those beans," she protested. Ada Hinton had nurtured the beans from seedlings.

Most of the furniture and cabinetry inside the Hinton home was built by the doctor himself. He was an expert cabinetmaker. He loved antiques, and Sunday afternoon outings with his wife and two daughters often included visits to antique shops in the Boston area.

Despite his interests at home, Dr. Hinton was always eager to get back to his laboratory and his test tubes. He was a completely dedicated scientist, and his medical work came first.

Ada Hinton seldom visited her husband's laboratory. When she did, it was to join him for the ride home to Canton at the end of his day. In addition to raising their two daughters, Mrs. Hinton spent much of her time in Boston working at Massachusetts General Hospital in the field of medical social work. She served as the vice president of the Boston Housing Foundation, president of the Community Fund in Canton, and vice president of the Home for Aged Colored Women in Boston.

In 1934, Dr. Hinton began writing his classic text, *Syphilis and Its Treatment*. For two years, the writing of the book was a night and day passion for the Hintons.

Ada Hinton was as much a driving force behind the book as her husband. She gave Dr. Hinton moral support and took over the household chores so that her husband could devote his full time and energy to writing.

William Hinton tried to provide, in his own words, "a clear, simple, relatively complete account of syphilis and its treatment for physicians, public health workers, and medical students." The book was warmly received upon publication in 1936. It was studied both in Europe and the United States as a unique contribution to the field of venereal disease. Drawing upon William Hinton's 20 years of research in the laboratory and hospital clinics, the book became a standard reference source in medical schools and hospitals.

Dr. Hinton made it very clear that diseases such as syphilis were "a by-product of poverty and ignorance and poor living conditions." Race, Hinton insisted, was not a determining factor.

Hinton's book documented his years of research and experience with patients. As his celebrated test for syphilis was a milestone in helping to conquer the disease, so his book was a milestone in medical writing on the subject.

A Giant of Medicine

Four years after the publication of his book, Hinton was involved in an automobile accident that changed the course of his life. The roads from his home in Canton to his laboratory at Harvard were icy on a cold November morning in 1940. As he drove alone to work that day,

Hinton's car skidded on the icy pavement and slammed into a stone wall.

Dr. Hinton climbed from his wrecked automobile and was hit and dragged along the road by another car. His right leg was badly damaged, and he was taken to the emergency ward at Boston's Peter Bent Brigham Hospital. Infection set in, and amputation of the leg was the only way to save Hinton's life.

The loss of his right leg caused Hinton chronic pain until his death, 19 years later. Nonetheless, during the last years of his life, he continued to teach at Harvard Medical School, the Harvard School of Public Health, and the Boston Dispensary.

Recognition came slowly and late to William Hinton. In 1946, he was promoted to the rank of lecturer at the Harvard Medical School. Three years later, a year before he retired and 22 years after he developed his test for syphilis, Dr. Hinton was elevated to the position of clinical professor. He was the first African American to attain the rank of professor at Harvard University.

Dr. Hinton was a modest man. Because he was so self-effacing, his achievements were not as widely known as they should have been. As a doctor, he believed that it was a scientist's duty to serve humanity, that the greatest reward for long hours of work in stuffy laboratories would be discoveries that would advance human knowledge and raise health standards. He disliked publicity and refused to promote himself on the basis of his contributions to medical science.

In addition to his natural modesty, William Hinton also felt that widespread knowledge that he was a black man would delay the acceptance of his test and book in the medical world. Most scientists and doctors interested in the field of syphilis knew that William Hinton was black, but he didn't want anyone to use his race as a reason for not accepting the merit of his accomplishments. For this reason, Hinton would not accept the Spingarn Medal from the National Association for the Advancement of Colored People (NAACP) when it was offered to him in 1938.

Dr. Hinton's fears about his test and book not being accepted because he was black were based on real concerns. Although the U.S. Public Health Service ranked his test above all others in 1934 and the American Serology Committee praised his test for its accuracy and simplicity in 1935, there was resistance to using it in some state health departments because it had been developed by an African American.

However, Dr. William Hinton's legacy to medicine and health care was not forgotten. In 1974, 15 years after Hinton's death, the State Laboratory Institute Building of the Massachusetts Department of Public Health was dedicated. The serology laboratory was named the Dr. William A. Hinton Serology Laboratory.

It was the laboratory he had headed for 38 years and where he had carried out his research. During his lifetime, Dr. Hinton probably would not have allowed the laboratory to be named after him, but it is a proper tribute to one of America's giants of medicine.

LOUIS T. WRIGHT

3

In the summer of 1911, a young black man by the name of Louis Wright boarded a train in Atlanta, Georgia. He was on his way to Boston to study medicine at the Harvard Medical School. Only a few weeks earlier, Wright had graduated from Clark College in Atlanta.

But his college diploma was not his only preparation for a medical education. As the train sped north, Louis Wright carried with him memories and experiences that would eventually produce not only a dedicated researcher and talented physician, but also a tough-minded fighter for the right of African-American people to receive quality medical care.

As a boy growing up in Atlanta, Louis Wright had seen racial injustice firsthand. He remembered the chain gangs of black prisoners who had built many of Atlanta's streets. The memory of those shackled and sweating men—the memory of the beatings and name calling against them—never left him.

When Louis was 15, a race riot broke out in Atlanta. His stepfather gave Louis a loaded Winchester rifle and said, "Son, you cover the front of the house. If anybody comes in that gate, let them have it. If you see they're going to get you, try to take two of them with you."

Louis was really frightened. He took his post in the front of the house. As the night wore on, he heard gunfire in the distance. In the bright moonlight, he could see the state militia marching up the road in front of the house. He saw his white neighbors take their guns and walk up the road.

Louis realized that he and his stepfather could not defend their home all by themselves. But he stood his ground at the front window. "Once you've faced death, you don't fear anything," he said later.

The family was saved by a white auto mechanic who drove them to a safer part of town. From this incident, Louis learned an important thing—he learned not to judge people by their color. It was a belief that sometimes made enemies for him among both blacks and whites in the years to come.

Louis Wright knew what it was to be a physician. His stepfather, Dr. William Fletcher Penn, was a doctor. Louis knew the step of the anxious father on the porch when a baby was due. He knew the worry that Dr. Penn felt as he nursed many people through a diphtheria epidemic. Louis knew the joy when a baby was born and the sadness when a patient died.

He knew that he wanted to be a physician.

What the Catalog Called For

No one could tell Louis Wright that he wouldn't find a way to use these boyhood memories and experiences. He believed in himself, perhaps more so because there were those around him who did not think black people could accomplish worthwhile things. That belief met its first major test at Harvard University.

The Harvard University admissions office was more than a little surprised to find that one of their applicants was a graduate of Clark College in Atlanta. To the Harvard admissions officers, Clark was one of those "funny little schools" that they felt certain could not prepare a person to enter Harvard Medical School. Not only that, but Louis Wright had not taken his chemistry exam.

The admissions office sent Wright to the office of Dr. Otto Folin, a Harvard professor and famous chemist. Quite a heated discussion took place in Dr. Folin's office. Louis Wright insisted that he be permitted to study medicine at

Harvard. Dr. Folin argued that Louis wasn't prepared for the study of medicine.

Finally, Dr. Folin asked, "Will you agree that if I ask you a few questions here today, I will never be bothered with you again?" Louis Wright agreed.

Dr. Folin then gave Wright an oral chemistry quiz. Wright passed successfully and was admitted to Harvard.

Louis Wright did well at Harvard, making such good grades that he won a scholarship each year. In the beginning of his third year, he faced his next big hurdle. It is in the third year that medical students begin to do actual work with patients.

When the assignments were given out, Wright was told that he could not go with his classmates to Boston Lying-In Hospital to learn to deliver babies (obstetrics). He would have to learn obstetrics, Wright was informed, from a black Harvard graduate who was practicing in Boston. "That's the way all the colored men get their obstetrics," said the instructor.

"I paid my tuition," said Wright, "and I want what the catalog calls for, namely, obstetrics at Boston Lying-In."

Wright got what the catalog called for.

Putting It on the Line

Wright was a senior at Harvard when he put at risk all that he had worked so hard for. The movie *The Birth of a Nation* was playing at the Tremont Theatre during the spring of 1915. It was considered by African Americans and some whites to be a racist, anti-black film. It gave an unfair picture of black Americans in the South after the Civil War.

Louis Wright joined the fight to have the showing of the film stopped. For three weeks, he cut classes and took time from his studying to march in the picket line in front of the theater in protest.

The pressure brought by the protesters resulted in a law that set up a censorship board that could ban films considered improper. The board did not ban *The Birth of a Nation* after reviewing it. Although the black citizens of Boston were not successful in driving the film out of the city, the protest had brought blacks and whites together to work for justice for African-American people.

On the day after the governor signed the censorship board bill, Wright returned to class. When he told his professor where he had been, the professor said, "I don't blame you. I think that's more important than your having been in my classes."

Finding a Hospital

Louis Wright graduated fourth in his class at Harvard Medical School in 1915. Now, he needed to find a hospital where he could serve his internship, a year of practical hospital work that is required before a medical graduate can be licensed to practice.

Once again, Louis Wright faced the problem of racial prejudice. "We've not taken Negro nurses, and we're not going to take Negro doctors," Wright was told at one hospital in Massachusetts.

"We've got troubles enough without adding the race problem," was another reply.

Louis Wright even tried the hospitals in Canada. From Vancouver General Hospital in British Columbia came this refusal: "I have no doubt in the world but what you would make an excellent intern in our hospital, but on account of your being a colored man I would be unable to take you on the staff."

Wright's stepfather suggested that he try Freedmen's Hospital in Washington, D.C. Freedmen's was the teaching hospital for Howard University, a black university.

Dr. Wright was accepted at Freedmen's and began his internship. It was at Freedmen's that Dr. Wright began his first real efforts in medical research. He had gotten a taste of research at Harvard while studying the effect of alcohol on the function of the stomach.

Dispelling Myths

A major health problem of the day was diphtheria. Diphtheria is a throat infection that can be fatal. The key to treating this contagious disease lies in prevention—that is, in giving susceptible persons a protective injection.

Two years earlier, in 1913, a Hungarian pediatrician, Dr. Béla Schick, had perfected a method of determining whether someone was susceptible to the bacterium that caused diphtheria. The test involved injecting a few drops of the diphtheria bacterium's poison, or toxin, into the skin. If the injected area became red and swollen after a few days and then turned brown, the doctor knew that the person lacked immunity to diphtheria. The test is called the Schick Test.

In medical school, Dr. Wright had been taught that blacks are more susceptible to diphtheria than whites. He had also read that the Schick Test was of little or no use in black people since it could not be read on brown skin.

A diphtheria epidemic among doctors, nurses, and patients at Freedmen's Hospital spurred Dr. Wright to put those two theories to the test. In his experiment, Wright gave the Schick Test to 207 black people and three white people. Skin color ranged from white to dark brown.

After a few days, Dr. Wright could see that the Schick Test *did* work on black people. While he couldn't always see the redness, there were other definite signs. The area near the injection area became slightly swollen, and the normally spidery-like lines of the skin grew thick and more definite. Silvery white scales formed in the area. Next, the area got darker than the surrounding area. On fair skin, the area turned light brown. On brown skin, the area turned black. Less than half of the black people tested proved to be susceptible to diphtheria, which is also the average for white people.

Dr. Louis T. Wright had made his first important contribution to medical knowledge. He wrote a report on his research and sent it to the *Journal of Infectious Diseases*. Dr. Wright's article was also the first published research to come from the staff of Freedmen's Hospital. It was not long before other doctors and textbook authors were quoting Wright's results.

"You Should Certainly Know Better"

Freedmen's was not free of racial problems, and Dr. Wright was always ready to respond to a racial insult. Once, he told a visiting U.S. senator not to call him "Sam." "It's time you learned to call a doctor a doctor," Dr. Wright informed the senator.

On another occasion, Wright told the commissioner of health to remove his hat in the women's ward. "You should certainly know better," said Dr. Wright.

When Dr. Wright finished his internship, he took the examination for his license to practice medicine, making the highest scores. As a licensed physician, Louis Wright went back to Atlanta to work with his stepfather.

But there, too, he was faced with the prejudice often shown to African Americans. One episode in particular brought Louis Wright face to face with a frightening part of himself.

The incident happened at the courthouse in Atlanta. Dr. Wright had gone there to register his medical license. An elderly white man took his license and told him to sit on the bench. As Dr. Wright sat waiting, he heard the man call, "Louie! Louie!" Dr. Wright didn't answer.

Then, the man came over and kicked Dr. Wright's foot. "I was talking to you," the man said.

"You're not talking to me," replied Dr. Wright. "I'm Dr. Louis T. Wright."

Next, the man called, "Wright! Wright!" Again, Dr. Wright told the man his name.

"You aren't going to try to sell any dope are you?" asked the man.

"Let me tell you something!" Dr. Wright shouted. "I'll choke you right here if you open your mouth again." At that moment, Dr. Wright really believed himself capable of violence. He simply could not take the disrespect that this man was showing him. Realizing how angry Dr. Wright was, the man quickly gave him his certificate.

Dr. Wright went home and told his parents what had happened. He was certain that it would be better for him to leave the South. He was horrified at the intensity of his own anger. But in the end Dr. Wright remained in Atlanta, for his stepfather needed him in the office.

Perhaps it was in Atlanta that Louis Wright reached the depths of his bitterness over the treatment of African Americans by white people. In later years, Wright's wife described this bitterness as she saw it in her husband:

> He had the same amount of bitterness that lots of people in the Negro race have, but he got over it in later life. He would say to me, "Bitterness doesn't pay. It frustrates your efforts to do things. It cuts your efficiency. Therefore, it is an evil thing. It is a destructive force."

While he was in Atlanta working with his stepfather, Dr. Wright began to pursue his special interest in surgery. He was appointed surgeon to Clark College, his old school. Wright did his surgery at the Fairhaven Infirmary, also in Atlanta, Georgia.

The year was 1917. Dr. Wright had been in Atlanta barely a year when the United States declared war on

Germany. With the entry of his country into World War I, Dr. Wright joined the Army. He was commissioned a first lieutenant and sent to Medical Officers Training Camp in Des Moines, Iowa.

A Better Vaccination

After his basic training, Lt. Wright was sent to Camp Upton, New York. He found medical work in an Army camp decidedly routine and monotonous. But he quickly found a way to make his work more interesting.

Lt. Wright was having a difficult time vaccinating the men against smallpox. When doctors vaccinate a person against smallpox, they inoculate a virus in between the skin layers. They then look for a "take" as an indication that the person has been made immune to the disease. The "take" is signaled by the appearance of tiny pimples at the inoculated spot on the arm. These tiny pimples get bigger and then break open and dry up. Eventually, a scab forms. It soon falls off, leaving a scar.

In 1917, there were three methods of placing the virus in between the layers of the skin. Each of these involved puncturing or scratching the skin of the arm and then rubbing the virus into the tiny wound.

Wright was using the official Army method of rubbing the virus into two scratches made with a sterile needle. But he was getting few "takes," even after repeating the vaccination many times.

Wasn't there a better way to place the virus into the skin layers? he wondered. Then, he thought of injecting the virus into the skin—intradermal or intracutaneous injection, it was called. It was much the same way that he had injected the toxin in his Schick Test research.

Selecting 227 volunteers (none of whom had shown a "take"), Lt. Wright tried out his new idea. On each man's arm, he tried the official Army scratch method and his new injection method. Of the 227 men, 160 had "takes" with the new injection method. But only 19 had "takes" with the scratch method.

Lt. Wright's new method seemed a much better way to vaccinate against smallpox. He reported the results to his commanding officer.

The Army immediately made Wright's procedure the official method of vaccination. Wright was recommended for promotion to captain. (He passed his promotion exam with a perfect score. But Wright's promotion was blocked by a commanding officer who refused to approve it.)

It was in New York that Dr. Wright met Corrine Cooke, the woman he was later to marry. His wife remembers their first meeting very well. "I met Louis, who was very shy, when I was selling tickets to raise money for an Army dance," she recalls. "He had watched me work and was impressed with what I was doing. He loved efficiency."

In June 1918, Lt. Wright landed with his regiment in France. He was made battalion surgeon and was put in charge of the surgical wards. Although he escaped the German bullets, Lt. Wright was caught in a poison gas attack. The attack put him in the hospital for three weeks. Afterward, Wright returned to his regiment, but the lingering damage to his lungs was to trouble him for the rest of his life.

On the day the war ended, November 11, 1918, the officer who had opposed Lt. Wright's promotion was transferred. Three hours after the officer left, his replacement signed Lt. Wright's promotion papers.

When he returned to the United States, Dr. Wright decided to settle in New York City. He now had a wife and a small daughter. (The Wrights would have two daughters, Barbara and Jane.) Once he had found a home and office, he decided to seek a position on the staff of a New York hospital. He filed his application with the New York Board of Hospitals.

"Have You Got a Vacancy?"

For years, black doctors had tried to get staff positions in the New York hospitals without success. When they filed their applications, they were told, "We'll let you know when there's a vacancy." But somehow there never seemed to be a vacancy.

Every day, Dr. Wright appeared at the board offices to check on vacancies. The answer was always the same: "You'll be notified, Dr. Wright."

This went on for six months, and it might have gone on for much longer had Dr. Wright not happened to meet Dr. Cosmo O'Neal, the superintendent of Harlem Hospital.

Dr. O'Neal knew of Dr. Wright's work with the Schick Test and smallpox vaccination. "I wish we could get a man like you in our outpatient department," he said.

"Have you got a vacancy?" asked Dr. Wright.

"We've been pitifully understaffed ever since the war," Dr. O'Neal said.

"Won't the board be glad to get this news? They've been looking for a vacancy for me," said Dr. Wright.

"You would consider it?" asked Dr. O'Neal. "When could you come?"

"When? Tomorrow morning," Dr. Wright replied.

And so Dr. Wright became the first black doctor to be appointed to the staff of a New York hospital. The barriers to black physicians had been broken.

But the battle was not over.

When Wright reported for duty, four staff physicians walked out. Two days later, Dr. O'Neal was transferred from the Harlem Hospital superintendency. He was made garbage inspector at Bellevue Hospital. Later, four more black doctors joined the Harlem Hospital staff. But when they came up for promotion, they were told by the hospital board that blacks could not be promoted. Any doctor who did not like the situation was invited to resign.

Dr. Wright did not resign. Instead, he renewed his fight. And he had not forgotten his friend Dr. O'Neal. He wanted to get justice for him as well as for other black physicians. Dr. Wright rallied his friends to protest the hospital board's policy.

News of the battle at Harlem Hospital made its way into the *New York News*, a black newspaper. Soon, black newspapers in other parts of the country picked up the story. People began to ask the mayor of New York what he was going to do about the Harlem Hospital situation. The National Association for the Advancement of Colored People (NAACP), of which Dr. Louis Wright was a member, also supported his battle. City Commissioner Ferdinand Morton, a friend of Louis Wright, used his influence with the mayor.

Finally, the mayor launched an investigation of the hospital board. As a result, the head of the hospital board was fired. The hospital was declared open to all qualified physicians, regardless of color. And Dr. Cosmo O'Neal was transferred from the Bellevue garbage yard to the superintendency of Fordham Hospital.

Dr. Wright was appointed to the surgical staff at Harlem Hospital. Now, he was able to build his skill as a surgeon. In 1929, he was appointed a New York City police surgeon, another first for a black physician.

Fighting Battles

In 1931, Dr. Wright found another battle to fight. He learned that the Julius Rosenwald Fund, an organization that provided money for worthwhile projects, was planning to build a hospital for blacks. In announcing the project, Edwin Embree, president of the fund, said that the hospital was needed to provide training for black doctors and nurses and to make health care available to black people.

Dr. Wright fought the planned new hospital by writing an eight-page pamphlet. In the pamphlet, he pointed out that such a hospital was not the solution to the black health care problem. "A segregated hospital makes the white person feel superior and the black person feel inferior," Dr. Wright argued. "It sets the black person apart from all other citizens as being a different kind of citizen and a different kind of medical student and physician—which you know and we know is not the case."

Wright continued his argument for racial equality in medical care: "What the Negro physician needs is equal opportunity for training and practice—no more, no less. Sick Negroes require exactly the same care as do other sick people. Segregated hospitals are always neglected. They represent a duality of citizenship in a democratic government that is wrong."

The pamphlet struck a fatal blow against the project. Not only was this hospital not built, but plans for other "black-only" hospitals were canceled.

That battle won, Dr. Wright turned his attention to treating the injuries that filled the surgical wards of Harlem Hospital. Gunshot wounds were becoming a more frequent problem for Harlem Hospital. With each new case, Dr. Wright learned more about such wounds. He learned how to tell the path of the bullet by studying the entry wound. He learned the value of restoring lost blood with intravenous fluids. He learned how to tell when surgery was necessary to repair the damage done by the bullet.

Another problem to which Dr. Wright gave his attention was bone injuries. One difficulty he faced was how to handle a patient with a broken or dislocated neck. Moving the person after the injury could cause the damaged bones to injure the spinal cord, possibly causing paralysis. Dr.

Wright could see that what was needed was a neck brace—and so he invented one. He needed a good way to treat severe fractures of the leg—and so he invented a special metal plate for splinting such injuries. Dr. Wright became such an expert on bone injuries, in fact, that he was asked to write a chapter on the subject in a medical book.

Dr. Wright was continuing his surgical work when he became very ill. A lung hemorrhage sent him to the hospital. His lungs, weakened by the gas attack during the war, had now become infected with tuberculosis. He was in the hospital for nine months.

Dr. Wright began to lose hope that he would ever get well. There was so much more that he wanted to do. The physician in charge of Dr. Wright's treatment felt that a change of scene might help, and so Dr. Wright was moved to a hospital in Ithaca, New York. There, in a room with a view of a lake, Dr. Wright's spirit began to be restored. His family, and former patients as well, made frequent trips to Ithaca. Finally, after three years at Ithaca, Dr. Wright was taken home.

Dr. Wright's heart had been permanently damaged by his long illness. His doctor had given him many rules to follow—no stairs and daily naps. He was not permitted to do surgery since the gases used for anesthesia were harmful to his lungs.

While still recovering, Wright was appointed chief of surgery at Harlem Hospital. Now, a new kind of life began for him. Restricted in his physical activity, he became a medical adviser, a trusted teacher, and a research leader.

As chief of surgery, Dr. Wright was able to take a hand in fulfilling his dream of making Harlem Hospital a true example of an interracial hospital. He refused to promote any physician on the basis of race. "I insist on the best man for the spot, white or black, Jew or Catholic," he often remarked. "And that's all there is to it." This policy cost him the friendship of some black physicians.

Dr. Wright insisted on the best work from all staff members. A young white intern quickly found that out. The intern was not interested in surgery, and he was sure that the standards of a city hospital would not be that high. He took little trouble with patient histories (brief summaries of past sicknesses the patient has had).

To the intern's surprise, Dr. Wright called him into his office. "Young man, henceforth you will write medical-school histories." Wright said. "Is that clear to you?"

For those whom he had to correct, Dr. Wright had this advice: "Accept your punishment, and go ahead and learn from it."

Dr. Wright set up a five-year surgery training program at Harlem Hospital. He urged interns to study surgery. Somehow, he managed to send the spark that had spurred his own ambition to many a young intern.

"Complete Integration"

It was during this time that Dr. Wright did most of his research. Such research involved everything from new ways to do surgical procedures to studying the dangerous side effects of certain medicines.

Perhaps Wright's most important research involved the first tests on humans of the antibiotic aureomycin. An antibiotic is a substance that kills disease organisms. Aureomycin had been tried on laboratory mice but never on humans. Dr. Wright tested aureomycin on the victims of a viral disease for which there was no known treatment. The patients were helped by the new antibiotic.

The year was 1949. Only a few years earlier, penicillin, hailed as the "miracle" antibiotic, had come into use. Now, it seemed that aureomycin was another "wonder drug." Dr. Wright tested the new antibiotic. It was found to cure such diseases as pneumonia, intestinal infections, typhus, and certain infections that sometimes followed surgery.

Cancer research was another important project undertaken by Dr. Wright in the late 1940s. He began to look for chemicals that would kill cancer cells without harming the cancer victim. He organized the Harlem Hospital Cancer Research Foundation.

By now, Wright's daughters were grown. Dr. Barbara Wright and Dr. Jane Wright (see Chapter 7) had become physicians, too. They joined their father in his research.

In April 1952, Harlem Hospital honored Dr. Wright by naming the new medical library after him. At the dedication ceremonies, Dr. Wright spoke with obvious pride of the institution that he had helped to build:

> Harlem Hospital represents the finest example of democracy at work in the field of medicine. Its policy of complete integration throughout the institution has stood the test of time.

Dr. Louis Wright's dream had been accomplished.

Several months later, in October 1952, Louis Wright died of heart failure. His research plans would have to be carried on by someone else. But Louis Wright left behind an important legacy: better medical care for all patients and equal opportunity for all physicians.

WILLIAM MONTAGUE COBB

4

The book was tattered and worn. A piece of white string held the pages within the binding. The once green binding was gray and scuffed. A dim light revealed the faint gold lettering on the book. It read, "The Animal Kingdom, Illustrated," by S. G. Goodrich. The book was the treasured possession of Dr. William Montague Cobb. Dr. Cobb carefully untied the string to reveal the faded inscription inside the cover. "This was given to my great-grandmother by my great-grandfather in 1871," he said.

The pages of the book are filled with descriptions of many animals. Detailed drawings show what many of the animals look like.

"My interest in animals began with this book," said Dr. Cobb. The young boy who was so interested in animals would grow into a man who became a leading anatomist, physician, teacher, and medical writer—as well as a strong activist for the rights of African Americans.

A Student of Living Things

Montague Cobb's native city of Washington, D.C., was full of experiences to learn from. "We were poor, but I didn't feel deprived," he often remarked. While the schools were racially segregated, Washington offered free concerts, zoos and aquariums, and art galleries.

To get to those places and activities, young Montague and his friends found that long hikes around Washington were often necessary. Those long hikes conditioned the future distance runner who was destined to break several records in college. Free concerts by the Marine band gave him an ear for music that later spurred him to play the violin in his leisure.

The zoo visits were Cobb's most vivid memories. His favorite animal was the rhino. To him, the rhino was an amazing sight. "It was an animal with tremendous tonnage. I knew that the skull itself weighed over 100 pounds. And it could move at speeds of 40 miles per hour. And yet, with all that weight, the rhino had control. That was really anatomy in action."

On other occasions, a young Montague Cobb would visit the Museum of Natural History. He would stare up at the skeletons of the dinosaurs and wonder why those animals had been unsuccessful. Why had they become extinct? The eohippus—that tiny ancestor of the horse—why had it galloped off into extinction?

Montague was bright—and that got him in trouble. When he skipped a grade in elementary school, he found himself the smallest boy in the sixth grade.

"I lost a lot of fights that year," Cobb recalled. He sent away for a book on boxing. During the summer, he used the book as a guide and taught himself how to box. As he began his seventh-grade classes, the bullies descended upon him again. But this time, he was ready for them. He threw a few of his newly learned punches. And things settled down.

At all-black Dunbar High School, Montague Cobb became a star athlete, winning two varsity letters (in track and cross-country) and a scholarship to Amherst College in Amherst, Massachusetts. At Amherst, he continued to make a name for himself in track, winning the intramural cross-country championship three years in a row. Montague also found a use for his seventh-grade boxing skills at Amherst, where he won both lightweight and welterweight titles.

Upon his graduation from Amherst, Montague Cobb was awarded the Blodgett scholarship for proficiency in biology. The scholarship meant that Cobb would spend the summer at the Marine Biological Laboratory in Woods

Hole, Massachusetts, a research institution where scientists and students gather to study marine animals.

Montague Cobb recalled this Woods Hole summer as one of his happiest. He studied embryology (the science that deals with the growth and development of living things) and attended lectures by the leading scientists of the time. Each morning, the students went out on the Woods Hole yacht and caught the specimens that they needed. Then, they studied the eggs and embryos under their microscopes.

Montague Cobb filled a thick notebook with sketches and descriptions of what he was observing. Cobb's finely detailed sketches showed, for example, the various changes that an egg undergoes when it is fertilized. Patiently, Cobb watched the changing egg through the lens of his microscope, drawing and describing the changes even as they occurred. In another series of detailed drawings, a microscopic view of a tiny fish was captured by Montague's careful pen.

Cobb received a certificate in embryology for his work at Woods Hole. But far more important to Montague Cobb was his newly gained skill as a laboratory biologist. For the first time, he truly felt that he was on his way to becoming a student of living things.

An Understanding of People

In the fall of 1925, Montague Cobb enrolled in the Howard University Medical School in Washington, D.C. He performed so well in his medical studies that, by his senior year, Cobb was appointed an instructor in embryology. Then followed a year's internship at Freedmen's Hospital.

There, Montague Cobb learned that an understanding of biology was not the only necessity for treating patients. He began to see that a good doctor had to combine his knowledge of medicine with a knowledge of people.

One patient whom Dr. Cobb was treating was very fat. In an effort to help her lose weight, Cobb had prescribed a customary daily dose of the laxative magnesium sulfate, also called Epsom salts. After a few doses, the patient told Cobb that she simply couldn't stand to take any more of that medicine.

So Cobb decided to try a dose of Epsom salts himself. It was so terrible that he canceled the laxative order. From then on, Dr. Cobb would try some of the less harmful medications on himself before he prescribed them.

Dr. Cobb had intended to begin practicing medicine as soon as he finished his internship for he now had a wife and small daughter. But he was urged by Dr. Numa Adams, dean of the Howard University Medical School, to spend several years studying anatomy with Dr. Thomas Wingate Todd, professor of anatomy at Western Reserve University in Cleveland, Ohio.

Under Dr. Todd's guidance, Dr. Cobb developed a view of human anatomy that would guide his future career. Todd rejected the idea that the study of anatomy was the mere memorizing of body parts. He believed that anatomy, since it dealt with the structure of the organism, was the basic biological science. Physiology was simply anatomy in action, pathology (the study of disease) was abnormal anatomy, and biochemistry was microscopic anatomy.

In 1932, after receiving his doctorate in anatomy and physical anthropology, Dr. Cobb returned to the Howard University Medical School, where he joined the Department of Anatomy as an assistant professor.

Like many good anatomy professors, Cobb began his teaching career with a simple goal in mind. Since anatomy was the basic science for physicians, he wanted his students to master it as they would any other skill. Anatomy, Cobb thought, should be as automatic as driving a car or playing a musical instrument. Students should know the structures of the human body without hesitation.

"He made you learn, . . . but he didn't teach," recalled Dr. Angella Ferguson, one of Cobb's students (see Chapter 9). "He could talk about animals and relate them to humans—and inspire you to go home and study."

Like Dr. Todd, Dr. Cobb felt that the mere memorizing of the names of muscles and bones and other structures was not the best way to study and understand anatomy. The student needed to understand how a muscle, for example, fitted into the organization of bodily functions. It was not enough to memorize the bones in the arch of the foot. How much better a lesson it was to approach the problem as one of mechanics: How does the arch function? What moves it? What supports it?

But by far Cobb's most important contribution to the teaching of anatomy was his concept of the X-ray eye. The X-ray eye enabled students to learn anatomy from the skin in. The student could look at an area on a patient's body and visualize the structures beneath the skin.

The two basic teaching tools used in helping students to acquire an X-ray eye were a human skeleton and a human cadaver (dead person).

The cadaver was propped up alongside the skeleton. Then, one of the students stripped off his shirt and stood next to the cadaver. By studying the bones of the skeleton and the structures inside the cadaver, the students outlined the structures of such organs as the heart and the lungs on the skin of their classmate. Mimeographed outlines of the body provided further practice toward training the X-ray eye. The students were learning "living" anatomy instead of the "dead" anatomy lessons learned by simply dissecting a cadaver.

Once his students had mastered the X-ray eye, Dr. Cobb taught them how to draw the body. He offered them an easy guide for getting the body proportions correct. The unit of measure is the head. The body should be seven and one-half heads high. The hipbone is the middle of the body. The nipples are two heads from the top and one head apart. The navel is three heads from the top. With those measurements as guides, students could easily add the other features such as arms and legs.

"No need to be an artist," Dr. Cobb told his students. "All you need is knowledge." He believed that drawing the body's structures was the best way to become familiar with them. "Drawing will also help you to find weak points or gaps in your knowledge of anatomy," he noted.

Dr. Cobb called his new method of teaching anatomy the "graphic method of anatomy." His approach received a commendation from the National Medical Association. A fellow anatomy professor at Howard commended Cobb's teaching method: "The more I listened to him, the more I learned," Cobb's colleague said. But perhaps the highest praise for Dr. Cobb could be found in the jammed lecture hall whenever he taught.

Montague Cobb made many other contributions to the Department of Anatomy at Howard. He began a museum that included examples of body features such as skull shape and breathing apparatus. He assembled a collection of more than 600 human and animal skeletons.

Dr. Cobb put the entire anatomy course on movie film. He did all the filming and editing himself. This provided the department with another unique teaching tool. The film could serve as an introduction to or a review of the anatomy course. In addition, Cobb started to collect color slides of many vital body structures, including microscopic views—another excellent teaching tool.

Dr. Cobb's teaching career at the Howard University Medical School spanned 48 years. More than 5,500 medical and dental students owe their knowledge of anatomy to Dr. Cobb. One student later became chief of surgery at Howard University Hospital.

"Leffall was his name," remembered Dr. Cobb. "He was one of my best students. I had a little custom in my anatomy classes that I called 'bust out.' I'd say, 'Who's ready for bust out today?' A student would say, 'Come on,

Doctor, try me.' Then, I would try to stump him with questions on material being covered in the classes. At some point, the student might be stumped—bust out. He would say, 'I'll be ready for you next time.' But Leffall—I could never bust him out."

Many years later, when Cobb had to undergo surgery, he insisted on having Dr. Lasalle Leffall as his surgeon. Leffall brought in a consultant and began to draw lines on Dr. Cobb's abdomen. "Never mind all those lines," said Dr. Cobb. "I want a diagonal incision, one that won't cut through too many nerves and won't show above my bathing trunks. And I want the fine hand of the master on this one. I want you to do everything."

"Remember, I'm the doctor here," said Dr. Leffall with a smile. "You stick to those cadavers."

Just before the operation, Dr. Leffall informed his old teacher that he was planning to do a diagonal incision.

"Work, Sweat, and Tears"

Even though he was busy teaching full-time, Dr. Cobb couldn't forget the days he had spent at Woods Hole. The memory of discovering and finally understanding a biological principle never left him.

Whenever he could get away to Cleveland, Dr. Cobb worked in the Western Reserve labs of his old professor, Dr. Todd. There, a huge anatomy collection was available. There were various skeletons, slides showing microscopic views of human tissues, and organs and other body parts preserved in formaldehyde.

For Dr. Cobb, the most interesting part of anatomy was the skeleton, the framework on which the soft body parts depend for support. The shape and the fit of the bones fascinated him. He was certain that each shape and each fit had a special purpose.

Dr. Cobb especially wondered about the bones of the head. What purpose did the shape of the bones of the face serve? Why, for example, did a camel have a rounded muzzle while a tiger had scarcely any nose at all?

As a graduate student working under Dr. Todd, Dr. Cobb had concluded that the growth of the upper teeth seemed to be one major force that shaped the upper jaw and the face. Cobb wondered how the growth of teeth produced so many differently shaped faces as occurred in mammals. He decided to study all of the mammals.

Approaching the problem the way an engineer might, Dr. Cobb studied the construction of 1,100 mammalian skulls. He asked himself several questions: What were the physical needs of the animals? How did the teeth serve those needs? How did the growth of the teeth help to shape the animal's face?

In his study, Dr. Cobb gave special attention to the rounded knobs on each side of the upper jawbone. These knobs, called maxillary tubers, are the place where the upper molars, or the grinding teeth, form. And the growth of that part of the bone seemed to play a major role in shaping the face.

When Dr. Cobb examined the camel skull, he found that the maxillary tuber grew out and back toward the base of the skull. Such growth gave the tuber little support. But the jawbone (to which the tuber was attached) thickened and grew forward, providing a strong foundation for the tuber and the teeth that developed. Thus, the camel has a rounded snout and many molars for grinding the grains and grasses it eats.

In the tiger skull, Dr. Cobb found that the maxillary tubers had grown sideways out from the head. The cheekbones and jaw joint were thickened to support powerful jaw muscles. The result was a V-shaped skull, one that was well designed for tearing flesh.

In humans, the maxillary tuber simply attached itself to the underside of the palate bone, producing a smaller face and a set of teeth suitable for eating many different kinds of foods.

Anatomy was not Montague Cobb's sole concern. He gave much attention to the problem of racial prejudice that plagued African-American people. Dr. Cobb felt that white prejudice against black people depended on the myth that black people were a biologically inferior race.

Montague Cobb attacked this myth by summoning all his knowledge of anatomy. He attacked with the facts.

In the 1930s, black athletes were breaking most of the records in certain track events, especially the short dash and the broad jump. As a result, the myth arose that black runners were good on the track because of some anatomical features that only black people had. One myth was that the heel bone of blacks was longer than that of whites, giving black athletes stronger feet.

Dr. Cobb exploded that myth in an article he wrote for the *Journal of Health and Physical Education*. Titled "Race and Runners," the article pointed out that "there is not a single physical characteristic which all the Negro stars in question have in common which would definitely identify them as Negroes." As proof, Cobb compared the physical measurements of some of the famous white and black athletes of the day.

In 1938, another doctor contended that "a split cartilage in the nose is a reliable test of Negro blood." Dr. Cobb wrote in *The Crisis*, published by the National Association for the Advancement of Colored People (NAACP), that "available anatomical knowledge indicates quite clearly that no cartilage is known to split in any human nose."

In 1941, addressing a black medical society at Tuskegee, Alabama, Cobb urged the physicians to mount an all-out attack on the myth of racial inferiority. How must this be done? "Work, sweat, and tears," was his answer.

Black doctors must educate themselves and convince others, Cobb said. He named several books that presented the facts about the biology of the black people. Only by arming themselves with the facts could they defeat the myths. Such facts had to be made available to government officials who made and upheld the laws of racial segregation. And black people had to be made aware of the facts so that their will to achieve would be stimulated.

Gradually, as he gave speeches and wrote articles, the anatomist also became a writer and a crusader for better medical care for black people. From 1949 to 1977, he served as the editor of the *Journal of the National Medical Association*, published by the medical society organized by African-American doctors in 1895. As the journal's editor, Dr. Cobb wrote hundreds of articles, including more than 200 biographies of African-American doctors.

In pamphlets, articles, and statements before the U.S. Congress, William Montague Cobb campaigned for better medical care for African-American people. Cobb founded and headed the Imhotep National Conference on Hospital Integration, an organization dedicated to removing racial discrimination in hospital care. He fought to guarantee the admission of African-American doctors to hospital staffs. In the course of his career, Dr. Cobb was named to more than 60 scientific boards, advisory councils, and medical activist organizations.

Honors to Montague Cobb came generously—medals, awards, and honorary degrees. He received the Distinguished Civilian Service Award, the highest award given to a non-military person by the U.S. chief of staff. For his accomplishments in the study of anatomy and physical anthropology, he was presented the Henry Gray Award, named for the author of the classic medical text known as *Gray's Anatomy.*

From the Medico-Chirurgical Society of Washington (the local branch of the National Medical Society), Cobb received a distinguished service award. "We never knew that Dad was receiving an award," recalled his daughter, Amelia Cobb-Gray, "until he asked to be driven to the award ceremony."

Perhaps Montague Cobb's most significant award was from the American Medical Association (AMA), the national medical society founded in 1847. It was not until around 1950 that African-American doctors were admitted to local affiliate medical societies of the AMA and hence to membership in the national organization. For years, Cobb had criticized the AMA for not opposing discriminatory health practices and for the organization's opposition to national health insurance.

On June 23, 1991, not long after his death, Cobb was posthumously awarded the AMA's Distinguished Service Award, an honor "given to a member of the Association for Meritorious Service in the Science and Art of Medicine." The award consisted of a medal and a $2,500 stipend. The stipend was donated by the Cobb family to the Howard University Medical School to fund an award for anatomy students, the Cobb Prize in Anatomy. The AMA award was accepted by Dr. Cobb's daughters, Amelia Cobb-Gray and Carolyn (Cobb) Wilkenson.

The greatest honor given to Dr. Cobb, however, was the esteem with which he was held by his students and medical colleagues, by his friends and neighbors.

In a commencement address at Morgan State University in Baltimore, Maryland, in 1964, Dr. Cobb observed "that everyone stands on so many people's shoulders that hardly anyone can take credit for anything." While that thought may be true, the work of Dr. William Montague Cobb—not only in science and research, but in civil rights as well—is something for which he alone can take credit.

Dr. Cobb retired from the Howard University Medical School in 1973, with the rank of distinguished professor. For the next 10 years, he plunged himself into civil rights and race relations work, serving as president of the NAACP from 1976 to 1982. The medical scholar and fighter for racial equality in health care now broadened his concern for "humankind" by leading the nation's pre-eminent and oldest civil rights organization.

In his last years, Dr. Cobb continued as a teacher, lecturing and speaking about the role and contributions of African Americans to medicine. During his lifetime, he had been the principal historian of the African-American contribution to medicine. Besides his biographies of black medical pioneers written for the *Journal of the National Medical Association*, Cobb also wrote a special issue of the journal in 1981 on "The Black American in Medicine."

Dr. Cobb described his understanding of the past and his hopes for the future by likening the black physician to a defensive lineman on a football team:

> They have to be rugged, tough, and determined. Their job is to make holes for fast backs to run through. If the backs are not there, the holes close up. Even when the backs are there, they have to fight their way for all the yardage gained. So it is for young black physicians today. They have enjoyed advantages unknown to their forerunners. . . . This increases their responsibility to make contributions in their own way.

In November 1990, Dr. William Montague Cobb died at 86 years of age. Memorial services were held at Howard University's chapel for this pioneer in American medicine.

ARTHUR C. LOGAN

5

"He was my doctor," said 80-year-old Frances Grant, sitting in the living room of her St. Nicholas Avenue apartment in New York's Harlem district. "Handsome, with shaggy white hair and piercing blue eyes—he was so warm to everybody. Wise in the ways of medicine, wise in the ways of surgery, he treated people. He knew enough about each of his patients so that he could always put them at ease. He could meet 'kings and cats' with no difference," said Frances Grant about her doctor and friend.

Dr. Arthur C. Logan was many things to many people.

- If you were a sick and elderly black woman living five flights up in a run-down tenement in New York's black community and you called Arthur Logan at three in the morning, he would come.

- When the Rev. Dr. Martin Luther King, Jr., was feeling down and in trouble, Arthur Logan was there. Logan was one of the few people who could be a pastor to Dr. King.

- When Duke Ellington, the great African-American jazz musician, lay sick in a Russian hospital, he telephoned Arthur Logan in New York and asked the doctor to come to his bedside. Arthur Logan packed his bags and traveled to Russia to be with his ailing patient.

- During the Poor People's March on Washington, D.C., in 1967, Dr. Arthur Logan put together a medical team to treat demonstrators camped out in tents.

- When blacks in Harlem picketed at local school construction sites to protest the lack of jobs for black workers, Arthur Logan was there, marching in line with the people of the community.

The name of Arthur Logan was almost a household word in Harlem, New York. Shortly after his death, Logan's name became a permanent part of the city when, in his honor, a New York hospital was renamed the Arthur C. Logan Memorial Hospital.

Remembering Dr. Logan

"The most important thing about Arthur," continued Frances Grant, "was that he was human. People could call him at any time of day, and he always took time to talk to them. I remember kidding him once when he was examining me in his office. He was taking my blood pressure with one hand and answering the phone with the other. I said, 'Now, don't get my blood pressure mixed up with somebody's telephone number.'"

In his office at West 139th Street, not far from Frances Grant's apartment, Dr. George Cannon remembered his long-time friend and associate. Outside Dr. Cannon's office, an ambulance, its siren screeching, speeds up the avenue. On its side, painted in gold letters, is its destination—the Arthur C. Logan Memorial Hospital. It is on its way to Convent Avenue and West 130th Street in West Harlem. Renamed for Logan in 1974, this private hospital had been known as Knickerbocker Hospital since 1856.

Dr. Cannon delivered the following tribute at Logan's funeral in November 1973:

> It has been my good fortune and an enrichment of my life to have known Arthur Courtney Logan since his childhood days when he played on West 130th Street and was a student at the Ethical Culture School. Our friendship and our professional lives have been intertwined ever since. From the very beginning, in the 1930s when we both opened offices to practice our profession, he showed great interest in the community. When Mayor La Guardia started the Health Insurance Plan, . . . he was among the handful who saw the need for a type of medical care that those with a limited income could afford. . . .

In any program involving community health, right up to the planned creation of a future Knickerbocker Hospital Medical Center, you would always find Arthur Logan giving advice, participating in, if not leading, discussions, and above all, knowledgeable about the subject, its current status in the city or state scheme of things, as well as its local importance. . . .

But Arthur was more than an organization man. The practice of medicine requires more than the scientific knowledge of health and disease in general. Arthur understood the art of practice as well. To him, a patient was not a case but an individual. . . . He knew his patients as individuals. . . . He loved his patients, and his patients loved him.

The Dream

During the last five years of his life, planning for a new Knickerbocker Hospital consumed much of Arthur Logan's time and energy. His goal was the creation of a community health center to replace both the 108-year-old private Knickerbocker Hospital and Sydenham Hospital, which was run by the city of New York. Both were old, run-down, and unable to meet the health needs of West Harlem, an area of nearly 30,000 people.

"Poor people just can't purchase the kind of health care they need and are entitled to," Dr. Logan insisted. "The community needs this health center badly. It will upgrade health services tremendously."

The new health center was to cover a six-block area. It was to include a 500-bed teaching hospital, a 200-bed nursing home, a 75-bed self-care unit, a mental health center, a medical office building for 40 doctors, a community recreation-social center, and over 1,000 low- and middle-income housing units. Dr. Logan was the driving force behind the project. It was his dream.

A Whirlwind of Activity

At 60 years of age, Dr. Arthur Logan was a prominent surgeon as well as a general physician. He had spent most of his professional life working on projects connected with the Harlem community. He was a staff surgeon at the city-run Sydenham Hospital.

Yet Logan still found time for shuttling back and forth between planning sessions for the new health center and meetings with government officials, representatives from businesses, bankers, and local and state politicians. Dr. Logan would attend meetings until well after midnight and still be in the operating room to perform surgery at seven o'clock in the morning.

Meetings and talks that were not finished during the day would go on at his home. "Well, drop by my house tonight," he would tell people, "and we'll continue." Often, people would arrive at Dr. Logan's West 88th Street home before he did and have to wait for him. His home was a whirlwind of activity, for anyone could come there for help or advice. It was the scene of numerous events to raise money for educational or social causes directed toward the improvement of conditions for black people or white-black relations in New York.

His day would start around six o'clock in the morning. Dr. Logan would cook himself a big breakfast of eggs, bacon, potatoes, and onions. He brewed a pot of coffee to drink while he read the *New York Times*. He would be in the operating room by 7:00 A.M.

Office hours followed surgery and hospital rounds. Patients came to the office during evening hours, too. At home, Logan was always busy. If he wasn't spending time with his son, who would stay up until his father came home, Dr. Logan would be reading the latest medical journal or surgical text. Often, he would fall asleep with a journal in his hands. He usually slept only four or five hours a night.

A Medical Background

Although New York City was Arthur Logan's home, his roots were in the deep South—Tuskegee, Alabama. His father, Warren Logan, was the first treasurer of the famed Tuskegee Institute, founded by Booker T. Washington in 1881. At age nine, Arthur Logan went to live with his older sister, Ruth, in New York. The move shaped his approach to life and his career in medicine.

His older sister was already a doctor when Arthur went to live with her. Her husband, Arthur's brother-in-law, was Dr. E. P. Roberts, the second black doctor to practice medicine in New York. He was also the first black doctor to serve on the Board of Health of New York City. In 1910, Dr. Roberts had been one of the founders of the National Urban League. Arthur Logan found himself growing up in a medical atmosphere and being raised by two people involved in civic affairs in the Harlem community.

From the Ethical Culture School in New York, Arthur Logan entered Williams College in western Massachusetts in 1926. Williams was a lonely place for Arthur and the six other black students enrolled there. It was his first exposure to racial prejudice by whites; but the bonds between Arthur and the other black students were strong, and they supported each other. In his junior year, Arthur Logan was awarded a Phi Beta Kappa key for excellent performance in his studies.

In 1930, Arthur Logan was in the freshman class at Columbia University's College of Physicians and Surgeons in New York. Four years later, he graduated with his medical degree, and from 1934 to 1936, he was an intern at Harlem Hospital.

"These were the real depression days," Logan once said, "the days of the first widespread, hard-core poverty among black people in New York City, and the days of a huge migration of black people from the rural South." The health problems of poor black people in Harlem were to become the problems that shaped Logan's life as a doctor.

In 1936, his sister and her husband were practicing medicine from a basement office on West 130th Street, in the center of Harlem. Upon finishing his training at Harlem Hospital, Logan moved in with them to begin his medical career. He worked from the West 130th Street office for six years before opening up his own practice.

Arthur Logan was a noted surgeon at Harlem Hospital from 1936 to 1962. He had been trained in surgery by Dr. Louis T. Wright (see Chapter 3). In 1969, when the surgical wing of the new Harlem Hospital Center was named in honor of Dr. Wright, Arthur Logan was one of those who paid tribute to Dr. Wright at ceremonies in the hospital auditorium. Logan said in his tribute to Wright: "I have been blessed not once, but three times in knowledge of and proud friendship—with Edward Kennedy Ellington, known as Duke, with Martin Luther King, Jr., and with the man whom we honor, although inadequately, today, Louis Tompkins Wright."

Dr. Logan was happy at Harlem Hospital, but he was attracted to Sydenham Hospital through his work with private patients. He was always concerned with the needs of the community, and when Harlem Hospital joined with Columbia's School of Physicians and Surgeons, Logan felt that the school would benefit more than the people of Harlem. So he resigned from the Harlem Hospital in 1962 and joined Sydenham.

Strong Friendships

Arthur Logan had a great number of friends from all walks of life. His friendship with the famed musician Duke Ellington was the most well known of these relationships. Dr. Logan would go around the corner or around the globe to care for Duke Ellington.

"Duke wouldn't cross the street without first asking Arthur," said Logan's sister.

Duke Ellington's band was playing at the Cotton Club in New York in 1947 when his lead saxophonist suffered a severe asthma attack before performance time. Ellington asked his road manager to find a doctor quickly. Dr. Logan was called to the Cotton Club, where he treated Ellington's ailing band member with an injection of adrenaline. In a few minutes, the sax player was breathing easily and was ready for the show.

Two days later, Ellington himself was feeling sick, and he remembered meeting Arthur Logan. He asked his road manager to make an appointment with Dr. Logan.

This was the beginning of a long friendship. Over the years, Logan tended to Ellington in such faraway places as Russia and India. Duke Ellington would call his doctor in New York from all parts of the world when he wasn't feeling well. Dr. Arthur Logan was Ellington's physician for 37 years.

Dr. Logan loved to entertain at his home in New York City. He would do the cooking. There was always a good time. There was good music and good food.

There were also serious conversations with Dr. Martin Luther King, Jr., Jackie Robinson (baseball's first black major-league player), and other leaders of New York City, both black and white. If someone wanted to raise money to fight drug abuse in Harlem, or help make Charles Evers the first black mayor in Mississippi, or send a black South African kid to college, Logan's doors were always open.

Arthur Logan would listen to any cause that would bring a better life for black and poor people in New York or anywhere in the country. When Logan passed away, Mayor John Lindsay praised him as a "leader of extraordinary intelligence and devotion, who somehow found the time and energy to express the widest range of social concerns while carrying the full load of medical practice and involvement in the medical community."

In Logan's home, there was a wall he called Martin's Wall. On it hung photographs of Martin Luther King, Jr., taken in Logan's home and on his various travels around the world. The civil rights leader was a close friend of the Logans. It was Logan's wife, Marian, who introduced her husband to King. Marian had been an active supporter and fund raiser for the black student sit-ins of the early 1960s. The civil rights leader and the doctor often debated political strategy when King visited the Logan home.

Personal Attention

Just as Arthur Logan had many friends, so he worked for an incredible number of social and civic causes. He volunteered his time and talents to city, state, and national groups. He was an active member in the NAACP Legal Aid and Defense Fund, the Harlem Urban Development Corporation, the National Urban League, the Harlem Youth Opportunities Unlimited (HARYOU), the National Medical Association, and the Southern Christian Leadership Conference—to name just a few.

"And he was an active member," said Dr. Kenneth Clark, HARYOU's first board chairman. "He wasn't just a name on our board list. He really cared about our work to get jobs and education for black youth. He gave the organization the kind of personal attention that he would give a patient."

Logan's deep concern for the health care of people with little income was always present. In 1948, Dr. Logan was one of the chief organizers of the Upper Manhattan Medical Group, a team of doctors who provided pre-paid, low cost medical care for the poor. Dr. Logan served as chief of surgery for this health clinic.

"He was an inspiration to people, particularly young people," remarked his wife, Marian Logan. "He was able to inspire other black youngsters . . . to get a good educational background so that they could become the best in whatever field they entered."

But Logan did not make a medical career sound easy. "He warned those who wanted to be doctors that medicine was hard work," Marian Logan added.

Logan dedicated the last years of his life to promoting financial and moral support for the Manhattanville Health Center, a medical center intended to replace Knickerbocker and Sydenham hospitals. Tremendous hurdles lay in the way of this project, including getting money to buy land near the old Knickerbocker facility. If housing had to be torn down to make room for the center, new housing had to be built for those whose homes would be taken.

Logan worked on the problems day and night.

There was a city bus depot a block away from the Knickerbocker, at Amsterdam and West 129th streets. If the huge garage were moved to another site, this site could be used for the new health center. Dr. Logan kept his eye on this location for several years, and in late November 1973, he learned that the bus depot could be relocated.

A possible new site for the bus terminal was 12th Avenue between 133rd and 134th streets. Arthur Logan went alone to view the location on a late November day in 1973. Tragically, it was to be his last day. He fell to his death from a point on the Henry Hudson Parkway, overlooking the site that perhaps would have helped to make his dream—a comprehensive health center for those who needed it most—a reality.

That dream never came true. The driving force behind it had been tragically lost. But the memory of this doctor—a doctor for all people—has not been lost. He has been remembered in many ways.

"Giant with a Gentle Touch"

Today, on the site of the old Knickerbocker Hospital, is Logan Memorial Plaza, between 130th and 131st streets at Amsterdam Avenue in Harlem. This 131-unit housing complex, completed in 1988, was dedicated "to someone who was more than a physician," said John L. Edmonds, the project's developer. The complex was named for a man, as Edmonds noted, who "watched out for the total needs of the community."

At Williams College, where Arthur Logan was one of only three African-American graduates in 1930, there is the Dr. Arthur C. Logan Memorial Scholarship, established in April 1974. The scholarship supports students who are in pre-medical studies.

Arthur Logan even appears in a story quilt created by the African-American artist Faith Ringgold. (Ringgold was commissioned to produce the quilt in memory of Williams College's first African-American graduate in 1889, Gaius Charles Bolin.) Stitched into the border around a blaze of lively colors on her quilt—"100 Years at Williams College, 1889-1989"—is a profile of Harlem's community doctor.

This man who was so many things to so many people is now remembered in many ways. But perhaps he is best remembered in the simple words of one of his patients. He was, for this patient and for many others, "a giant with a gentle touch."

DANIEL A. COLLINS

D aniel Collins was born in the small town of Darlington, South Carolina. He was born into a world
of work. His mother taught school and ran a family-owned
neighborhood grocery store. Daniel's father had his own
heavy equipment company that transported houses, tim-
ber—anything that was heavy and needed moving.

His parents' labors produced an important reward for Dan—a good and loving home. It was a home to grow up in, a place where a young person could feel safe and secure. Looking back from adulthood, Dan Collins would often say that it was there, in that home, that he learned to use the best that was in him.

When he was old enough, Dan learned about work, too. He worked as a gardener. He sold newspapers. He worked for a butcher, cleaning and selling fish. He used the best that was in him. And there was a lot of that. Dan Collins grew up to be a dentist, research scientist, health educator, writer, editor, and corporate executive.

But had Dan Collins the teen-ager been able to look into the future and see Dan Collins the adult, he might have been quite surprised. For there would be many a twist and turn to his life.

A Slow Start

Dan Collins couldn't have enjoyed his years at Mayo High School. At 236 pounds, he was nearly as wide as he was tall. His classmates teased him. Girls ignored him. And what was worse, Dan agreed with them. All of this added up to an unhappy Dan Collins.

Dan showed his unhappiness by throwing spitballs and talking in class. He studied only enough to get by. But his family expected him to stay in school and go on to college, and so he stuck it out.

There was one good thing about his size. Dan was a star on the football team. When a teacher gave him a failing grade, Dan thought that he deserved better. After all, he was a football star. He came up with a good way to get even with the whole school. Dan decided that he would turn in his football uniform. That would fix them, he thought. They wouldn't win any more games.

Dan was really getting off on the wrong track.

Then, he met I. C. Wiley, a math teacher at Mayo High. Dan always had a talent for math. Even without studying, he often did well in class. Wiley encouraged Dan to work harder on his math. Dan was soon leading the class. The taste of success spurred him to work harder in his other classes.

Dan Collins was beginning to believe in himself. It was an important step for him. By the time he entered Paine College in Augusta, Georgia, Dan had become a good student. He chose chemistry for his major subject.

Dan did so well in chemistry that he was made a laboratory assistant. This meant that he was responsible for seeing that the equipment and chemicals were ready for the students. He was also given his own chemistry projects to do. Dan began to see how much more there was for him to know. The first seed was planted in the mind of the future scientist.

Chemistry was not the only thing Dan Collins learned at Paine College. He also learned some important things about people.

Throughout his school years in Darlington, Dan had never had a white teacher. At Paine, half the faculty was black and half was white.

Later, Dan was to write about this experience in a church magazine:

> By the time I entered Paine College as a freshman, I had hardly ever encountered a white person whom I could identify as friendly or who had any concern for me or my kind beyond the immediate business at hand. . . . In 1932, had I known about the interracial commitment at Paine College, I might have been too terrified of southern whites to become a part of that freshman class. . . .
>
> Paine College proved to be an oasis in a desert of poor race relations. It was there that I met intelligent, concerned and dedicated white southerners who . . . accepted my feelings of human equality. It was there that I began to know that white and black people had much more in common and much more to share than not. The black and white teachers . . . helped to strengthen my ailing self-image, a great need growing out of the heritage of any southern black male. Even in the early 1930s, on the Paine campus I never once was made conscious of my blackness or felt the need to recognize another's whiteness.

Dan Collins completed his studies at Paine College in 1936. He had done so well in college that his professors urged him to study chemistry in graduate school. But Dan couldn't see himself as a chemist. He wanted to be a construction engineer. He planned to work with his father, building bridges and highways.

To get a taste of construction work, Dan went to work for his father after completing his college education. His father worked across the entire state of South Carolina on projects that might take weeks to complete. So Dan and his father could not come home each night after a day's work. Dan's father would rent a house near his job, and the crew would live there until the job was finished. Sometimes, they would get home on weekends. But it was a camp life, and Dan didn't care much for it.

Something had also happened while Dan had been away at college that made him change his mind about being a construction engineer. During Dan's high-school years, his father had been his own boss. Mr. Collins was the outstanding house mover in the state. But when the state began a big highway construction program, it set up its own house-moving division.

This meant that Daniel's father was forced to work under state officials. People who had no experience at all were now his father's bosses, simply because Mr. Collins was black and they were white. It didn't bother the father too much; he was used to it. But it was a blow to the son. Out of his unhappiness and disappointment came the idea to become a physician.

"I'll Take It"

Daniel Collins applied to two black medical schools, Howard University Medical School and Meharry Medical College, but there were no openings. However, Meharry, in Nashville, Tennessee, said that there were some openings in dentistry. "I'll take it," Daniel Collins wrote back.

Collins' grades at Meharry were outstanding. Projects that involved vitamin research increased his interest in further study. After graduation, Dr. Collins was offered a chance to study at the Guggenheim Dental Clinic in New York City. There, he was trained in dentistry for children.

Research on tooth decay in children was taking place at Guggenheim, and Collins had a part in that.

Dr. Collins had just finished his year at Guggenheim when he was offered a chance to do post-graduate study at the University of California in San Francisco, California. There, he could devote his full time to research, something that Collins found more and more interesting. He wanted to get his master's degree in dentistry and then go back to Meharry, where he planned to settle into a career of teaching and research.

At the University of California, Dr. Collins began to study and do research under the guidance of Dr. Hermann Becks, a physician and dentist who headed the division of dental medicine. The division studied the cause of tooth disease and the prevention of tooth loss.

Dr. Collins was awarded his master's degree in dentistry in 1944. In the months before he earned his degree, Dr. Collins had been exchanging letters with officials at Meharry about his joining the faculty there.

Although Meharry had a black student body, the top administrators and many of the instructors and professors were white. Quite by accident, Collins learned that black instructors were paid less than white instructors of the same rank. "I could not live with that," he remembers. "People may be superior to me because of certain abilities but not because of skin color."

The president of Meharry wrote that if Dan Collins came back to his old school, he would have to accept things as they were. Dr. Collins decided to stay at the

University of California. He was appointed an instructor in the College of Dentistry and continued working under Dr. Becks. Collins and Becks worked with another leading researcher, Herbert M. Evans, who headed the Institute of Experimental Biology.

In the Laboratory

Out of Evans' lab had come a good deal of important research. The significance of human chromosomes was being studied there. (Chromosomes are threads of protein and nucleic acids within the body's cells that direct the transmission of hereditary traits.) In the Evans lab, it had also been discovered that Vitamin E is essential for the reproduction of mammals. Important research was being done on how chemicals called hormones control many vital functions in the body. Dr. Collins felt truly honored and fortunate to be working here.

Much of Dr. Evans' hormone research was done on laboratory rats. The gland known to produce a particular hormone was removed from a rat. Then, research teams studied the effects of the hormone deficiency on different parts of the body. Some teams looked at the long bones; others studied such organs as the kidneys, heart, and lungs. Dr. Collins was on the team that studied the head, face, jaw, and teeth.

In one project, Dr. Collins studied the effect of the lack of certain hormones on the temporomandibular joint (the jawbone joint) and other dental tissues. The proper functioning of this joint is crucial to the health of the teeth. A diseased or injured jaw joint can cause the teeth to grind abnormally against each other, producing pain and damaged teeth.

So that he would know what to look for, Dr. Collins studied the jawbone joints of normal rats of different ages (ranging from five days to four months). The mice were first killed; then, X-rays were taken of the jaw joint. Next, very thin slices of the jaw joint were made and placed on slides. These slides were then examined microscopically.

As he studied the jaw joint in normal rats, a pattern of growth and development of the joint began to emerge. In the youngest rats, the rounded end of the jawbone was made up of cartilage.

Gradually, as the rat grew older, more and more of the cartilage was replaced with bone cells, until only the very outer part of the bone end remained cartilaginous. As more and more cartilage was replaced by bone, the joint was less able to withstand the stress of disease and injury.

Next, Dr. Collins studied rats whose pituitary gland had been removed by surgery. The pituitary, located at the base of the brain, is sometimes called the master gland. The pituitary produces many hormones that regulate vital body processes. One hormone produced by the pituitary is called growth hormone. This hormone is known to regulate the growth and development of many bones. But no one knew much about the effect of growth hormone on the growth of the jawbone. By studying rats who lacked a pituitary gland, Dr. Collins could find out what the lack of growth hormone might do to the jaw joint.

Collins studied the jaw joint of rats without pituitary glands, using the same procedure as before. Studies were made on rats after their surgery. What Dr. Collins saw was a very rapid aging of the jaw joint. The jaw joints of those rats who had gone without growth hormone had rapidly progressed to the final stage of aging normally found in much older rats.

The research seemed to show that growth hormone did affect the jaw joint and, hence, dental health. But Dr. Collins needed more proof. To prove his theory, Dr. Collins injected the hormone into another group of rats whose pituitary glands had been removed. Like the other group without pituitary glands, the jawbones of these rats were severely aged.

The growth hormone had a dramatic effect on the ends of the aging jawbones. The bone ends began to thicken with cartilage. After hormone injections, the bones had been restored to a healthy, youthful state.

This experiment with hormone injections proved that the pituitary gland did, in fact, play a role in dental health. Another bit of knowledge was now available, and the study of pituitary function became an important diagnostic tool for the dentist.

What effect did the pituitary gland have on teeth? Studies of rats without pituitaries revealed the answer. The structure of the tooth began to break down. The pulp, or inner core containing the blood circulation system of the tooth, began to shrink. Holes appeared in the hard outer enamel layer, and the tooth became misshaped.

For Dr. Daniel Collins, this was the high point of his research. The discovery that removing a gland could control the growth of a tooth was very exciting to him. He had found an important factor determining dental health.

A medical fad in the 1940s led Dr. Collins to his next research project. The fad was Vitamin D. Vitamin D was supposed to cure everything from colds to tuberculosis. People were flocking to drugstores, where they could buy big bottles of capsules without a prescription.

University of California nutritionist Dr. Agnes Morgan asked Dr. Collins to study the physical effects of huge Vitamin D doses. Testing large doses on dogs revealed the great hazard of such large vitamin doses.

Dr. Collins found that Vitamin D stimulated the movement of calcium from the bones into the blood stream. Then, when the vitamin dosage was stopped, the calcium spilled out of the blood stream into the body's tissues. The calcium clogged the blood vessels in vital organs like the kidneys and lungs. Tissue deprived of blood circulation died. Calcium also hindered circulation within the pulp of the teeth, causing them to become distorted and weak.

Other scientists were finding that the vitamin was particularly harmful to children. When the reports of Dr. Collins and the other scientists were released, the action of the U.S. government was swift. The Food and Drug Administration (FDA) issued orders that the amount of Vitamin D added to milk be reduced. The FDA also ruled that only regulated amounts of Vitamin D could be sold without a prescription.

Success Stories

In addition to his medical research, Dr. Collins also treated patients in his dental office. One case history he has always saved.

It tells the story of two small boys afflicted with an inherited disorder called ectodermal dysplasia. Something had gone wrong with their development before birth, and they were born with body defects. They had only wispy eyebrows and hair; they had very high foreheads. Their classmates made their lives miserable, and the boys were doing poorly in school. Another problem was that the boys had no sweat glands. The evaporation of perspiration cools the body during hot weather. Deprived of a natural cooling system, the boys developed high fevers and convulsions during hot weather.

When the boys walked into Dr. Collins' office, they were hoping for a solution to a different problem—they wanted teeth. One boy had only two teeth. The other had six stubby teeth. Dr. Collins examined the boys. Then, he made models of their mouths and had upper and lower dentures made for them.

Photos in the boys' case history file show the result. The "before" photo shows two solemn-eyed boys. One has the sunken mouth of a person with no teeth. The "after" photo shows two smiling, apparently normal boys.

"When I put in their teeth, their eyes lit up, and they gave me a big hug," said Dr. Collins. "That was the biggest paycheck I ever got."

Having teeth made a big difference in the lives of the two boys. They could eat and speak better. They began to do better in school. One brother became an Eagle Scout. Fitting the boys with teeth was a simple solution to a serious problem.

But the diagnosis and treatment of dental problems is not always so simple. A major problem in dentistry is finding the reason for pain of the jaws, teeth, and face. In fact, the problem of pain so intrigued Dr. Collins that he went to the medical library and read every research paper he could find on the subject. He found that there was a great deal of information on pain, much of it not taught to dental students.

Pain is the result of the activation of a nerve cell. The pain message travels along the pathways of the nervous system to the brain. When the message reaches the brain, the person feels the pain. Dr. Collins found that several different problems can activate the pain impulse. Often, the problems narrowed down to a malfunctioning of the blood vessels and muscles or irritation and inflammation of the teeth and jawbone.

To help patients with unexplained pain, Dr. Collins and another dentist organized the Consultative Oral and Facial Pain Service at the University of California Dental School. Patients who came to the service were first asked many questions about their pain: how the pain felt, when it happened, what seemed to bring it on, and what seemed to help it. X-rays and a physical examination of the jaw, the mouth, and the neck were done.

One woman was found to be grinding her teeth while sleeping. This irritated the muscles of the jaw and neck and produced the pain. She was given a special splint to wear over the lower teeth at night. This prevented her unconscious tooth grinding. Within four days, she began to get relief from the pain.

Not all people who brought their pain to Dr. Collins were so successfully treated, however. One man came in with such severe facial pain that he could not even bear to wash his face. One of Dr. Collins' associates was able to stop the pain by injecting alcohol in the nerve to stop the pain impulse. But the doctors were never able to find the cause of the pain.

"Set Me Up a Research Program"

Dr. Collins' work at the University of California was interrupted in 1956 by a call into the Army. After basic training, he was assigned to the Armed Forces Institute of Pathology at Walter Reed Hospital in Washington, D.C.

At the time, the Dental Division of the Armed Forces Institute of Pathology was under the command of Colonel Joseph Barnier. "Set me up a research program"—this was the order that the colonel gave to Dr. Collins.

The first project begun by Dr. Collins involved testing the effects of a recently developed way for dentists to grind teeth. The new method, called high-speed instrumentation, was fast and not as uncomfortable as the old method of grinding. But some dentists were concerned that this technique might harm the delicate nerves within the tooth.

Dr. Collins and the other members of the staff set up an experiment with dogs in which the effect of high-speed instrumentation on nerves could be tested.

Dr. Collins also began to study the cancers that might affect dental health. He was continuing his pain research as well. As a top staff member, he had the chance to work with many other pathologists, studying the cause and the effect of disease in dental and gum tissue.

Pathology (the study of disease) taught Dr. Collins the different kinds of things that can happen to a nerve. He learned that cut nerves can form a tiny swelling, called a neuroma, on the cut end.

The neuroma can trigger pain. It is this phenomenon that produces the so-called "phantom pain," pain that a person feels, for instance, in an amputated arm or leg. Neuromas on cut nerves in the mouth can also produce strange, difficult-to-diagnose pain.

By 1958, Dr. Collins had finished his Army service. He headed back to California, full of ideas for research that he would like to undertake. The University of California, with its modern laboratories, was an ideal place to do research in dentistry.

Disappointments and Rewards

Dr. Collins thought that he had earned a promotion to a permanent position on the university staff. As an associate professor, he could conduct his own research. He would have more assistants and more lab space to study dental science.

Collins had taught on the University of California dental faculty for 16 years. He had 25 articles of published research to his credit. He had received honors and awards for his research. He had a graduate degree and a certificate from the oral pathology board, in addition to his dental degree. He had written chapters for dental textbooks.

Dan Collins felt that he was well qualified to be an associate professor.

Still, Dr. Collins wasn't sure how the university would respond to his promotion request. He would be the first African American with the rank of associate professor. A close friend who was Jewish had pushed for promotion a year earlier. He, too, was well qualified. But no Jew had ever been appointed to the rank of associate professor on the dental faculty. The friend did not make it. And Dr. Collins' promotion was also turned down.

This treatment marked a low point for Collins. He could see that he was as well qualified as any of the other associate professors in the dental school. The injustice hurt deeply. Collins' university career had come to a dead end. He saw all his research coming to an end as well. Would anyone learn more about his discoveries? And what about the new ideas that he wanted to try? What would happen to them?

After he left the university, Collins established his own full-time private dental practice in San Francisco. He was in private practice until he retired in 1976.

Collins' patients reaped the rewards of those many years of research. One woman was especially fortunate to have brought her problem to Dr. Collins. For six months, she had been troubled with pain in the upper left face. She had been to many dentists and physicians. But they had done little for her except to give her prescriptions for more painkillers.

Collins looked into the woman's mouth and almost at once pinpointed the problem. There was a large and painful swollen area in the left side of the roof of her mouth. It looked like cancer of the maxillary sinus. Lab tests confirmed the diagnosis. Treatment meant cutting out part of the roof of the woman's mouth. The woman refused to have the disfiguring surgery. "I'm going to travel," she said, "and think."

Six months later, the woman agreed to the surgery. But she had lost precious time. The cancer had grown, and the possibility that it had spread to other parts of the body was also greater. She came through the surgery well, however. She was fitted with an artificial palate and was soon able to eat and speak.

A Chance to Work for Children

Dr. Collins began to devote more time to community service. He was appointed to numerous commissions and boards, such as the mayor's committee on youth and the California State Board of Public Health. Dr. Collins also received a presidential appointment to the National Health Resources Advisory Committee. But the appointment that changed Collins' life was the one that named him to the California State Board of Public Education.

"Here was a chance to work for all the 4 million kids in California," Collins said.

Collins himself had four sons, and he had seen the textbooks that they used in school. There was something that had always bothered him about those books. Black people were shown as inferior and non-achieving people. True, Booker T. Washington, George Washington Carver, and Jackie Robinson were in the books. But beyond that, there was little to admire about the black people presented in the textbooks.

Being on the education board was a chance to do something about the content of public-school textbooks. After talking to publishers, the board decided to take a hard look at the kinds of books that California would buy. The board asked the Department of History of the University of California to study the textbooks being used by California students. The study showed that many different kinds of people were unfairly depicted in the books.

The result was that the board, with the backing of the governor, pushed through a new law. The law said that California would not accept any book that did not include a fair representation of ethnic groups and women.

The textbook publishers soon began to change their books. One publisher wrote a completely new history book that showed the contributions of many different kinds of people. Despite several attacks on the textbook, it was eventually accepted in many other states. Many publishers began to look to California for guidance on what books the education departments of the states would buy.

In 1968, Daniel Collins wrote his own book, titled *Your Teeth: A Handbook of Dental Care for the Whole Family*. Dr. Collins also wrote several articles on dentistry for the Encyclopedia Americana Science Supplement. Two years later, in 1970, Collins was asked to head a newly created division of a textbook publishing company, Harcourt Brace Jovanovich (HBJ).

Changing the Books

Daniel Collins gradually reduced the amount of time that he spent in his dental office and gave more time to publishing. He was full of ideas that he wanted young readers to understand.

"I want the student to learn to love himself. I want him to learn how to make decisions," Collins remarked. "I want to inform him of the things that will endanger him. I want him to understand that many diseases are determined by lifestyle—rest, food, hygiene, etc."

Collins wanted his young readers to take charge of their health. "There is no way a doctor can keep up with all the diseases a person can produce for himself," he said. "Each person must learn how to prevent disease and how to maintain good health."

Collins began to produce a series of health textbooks for students in kindergarten through junior high. From 1972 to 1976, he worked half-time for HBJ. He shuttled back and forth between his dental office and HBJ's Division of Urban Education in San Francisco. Often, he would have to travel to HBJ's New York City headquarters.

In 1976, he retired from his dental practice and went to work full-time for HBJ.

Dan Collins kept his license to practice, however, for, as he once remarked, "one never knows what life holds in store." In 1981, Dr. Daniel Collins, the dentist-turned-publisher, retired from his publishing career.

"Hard Work and Solid Achievements"

The life of Daniel Collins is a record of commitment and achievement as a dentist and health educator. Beginning in 1968, he started serving as the chairman of the Board of Trustees at Paine College, where he had started his professional training in 1932.

For his years of dedicated work for Paine as a trustee, the college named its new library, dedicated in October 1991, the Collins-Calloway Library. (Dr. Morgan Calloway was the first president of Paine in 1882.) Dr. Collins was also a trustee of Meharry Medical College for many years. In May 1991, he was made an honorary Doctor of Humane Letters during his fiftieth class reunion.

In addition to serving the two colleges that prepared him for a medical career, Dr. Collins has been an active member of many other organizations—the National Urban League (where he served as vice president of the board), Radio Free Europe, Natomas Company (one of California's largest corporations in mining, oil exploration, and shipping), the California State Board of Public Health, and, as mentioned, the California State Board of Education, to name a few.

In a 1982 interview, Dr. Collins explained why he felt it was so important to make a contribution to the welfare of the community:

There is a fulfillment that one gets in giving back to his or her community that more than compensates for the time and energy you give. It gives you a sense of direction for your own life, and it gives you a feeling of self-worth that does not come along with being a successful accountant or a successful dentist. . . . It rounds out one's life and pays back in big dividends. So you really aren't giving anything: you're investing . . . not in hard capital, but investing something of yourself into your community. It is very important.

Dr. Collins' life and work has often gone in directions that he had not envisioned or planned. But he believes in taking an opportunity and, as he says, "running with it." He once said, "My parents inspired me to respect hard work and solid achievements, and to work for the betterment of society."

Dan Collins has faced a world of racial discrimination and limited opportunities for African Americans. But his parents' teachings and example made it easier for him to cope with whatever problems he faced.

In addition to the influence of Andrew and Lucy Collins, Dr. Collins had a spiritual mentor and personal friend in Dr. Howard Thurman (1900-1981). Dr. Thurman was an African-American religious leader who co-founded the interracial Church for the Fellowship of All Peoples in San Francisco in 1944.

Dr. Thurman wrote a poem called *The Threads in My Life* that Dan Collins often recited. It is a poem that tells

us a great deal about the inner life of Dr. Daniel A. Collins.
The poem reads in part as follows:

Only one end of the threads,
I hold in my hand
The threads go many ways,
linking my life with other lives . . .

One thread comes from a high flying kite;
It quivers with the mighty current
of fierce and holy dreaming
Invading the common day with far-off places
and visions bright . . .

One thread comes from the falling
hands of an old, old friend
Hardly aware am I of the moment
when the tight line slackened
and there was nothing at all—nothing . . .

One thread is but a tangled mass
that won't come right;
Mistakes, false starts, lost battles,
angry words—a tangled mess
I have tried so hard,
but it won't come right . . .

One thread is a strange thread—
it is my steadying thread,
When I am lost, I pull it hard
and find my way.
When I am saddened, I tighten my grip
and gladness glides along its quivering path;
When the waste places of my spirit
appear in avid confusion,
the thread becomes a channel
of newness of life.

One thread is a strange thread—
it is my steadying thread.
God's hand holds the other end.

JANE C. WRIGHT

7

It must have seemed only natural for Jane Wright, the daughter of Dr. Louis Wright (see Chapter 3), to study medicine. Her father was an accomplished and famous physician. What better thing to do with her life than to follow in his footsteps?

Jane Wright remembers her father's influence every step of the way. Once, as a medical student, she was struggling to learn the life cycle of certain worms and other human parasites. Her father amazed her by reciting life cycle after life cycle. As a New York physician, he seldom had contact with parasitic diseases, which are common in tropical areas. And yet he remembered the exact details of those life cycles.

For more than 35 years, Dr. Jane Wright has conducted medical research in the use of chemicals to treat the disease of cancer in humans.

While her father's dedication to and achievements in medicine had impressed her, swimming and art captured Jane's interest and talents during her high-school and college years. At the Fieldstone School in New York City, she was captain of the swimming team. Jane Wright broke school records for both the 100-yard freestyle and 100-yard breast stroke. She also served as the editor of her high school's yearbook.

Entering Smith College in 1938, Jane became an outstanding varsity swimmer. Jane set college records that would go unbroken for many years. By the end of her sophomore year, however, Jane Wright's early love for art and her desire to be a painter were replaced by an interest in the sciences.

Jane Wright had decided to become a doctor.

In 1942, Wright was one of two women in Smith's graduating class to be admitted to medical school. She won a four-year scholarship to New York Medical College. The scholarship was a blessing since her father was hospitalized with tuberculosis at that time; the strain on family finances would have prevented a medical-school education for Dr. Wright's daughter.

After earning her medical degree in June 1945, Wright interned at New York City's Bellevue Hospital and then served as an assistant resident doctor in internal medicine until 1947. She then moved on to a year's residency in internal medicine at Harlem Hospital.

In choosing a medical specialty, Wright gave thought to her personal life. She did not select surgery or obstetrics because these specialties require doctors to be on call 24 hours a day. While she knew that her days as a physician would be long, a regular and scheduled life—the kind of life that would enable Wright to raise a family—was also important to her.

In 1947, Wright married David D. Jones, a lawyer, and within a year, their first daughter, another Jane, was born. In July 1948, after a six-month maternity leave, Dr. Wright returned to Harlem Hospital as a chief resident to complete the last stage of her medical training. A second daughter, Alison, was born in 1950.

For the first six months of 1949, Dr. Wright worked as a New York City school doctor and a visiting physician at Harlem Hospital. But wanting more of a challenge, she accepted a position in June 1949 as a clinician at the Harlem Hospital Cancer Research Foundation established by her father.

It was here that Jane was introduced to research that involved the effects of drugs on cancer tumors and other forms of abnormal cell growth in the human body. When her father died in 1952, Jane Wright succeeded him as director of the cancer research center.

Pioneer in Chemotherapy

Normally, the cells that make up the body reproduce in an orderly manner so worn-out tissues are replaced, injuries to the body are repaired, and growth of the body proceeds. Occasionally, however, certain cells undergo a change that is abnormal and thus begin a process of uncontrolled growth and spread. These cells may grow into masses of tissue called tumors.

The danger of cancerous tumors is that they can invade and destroy normal tissue. In the beginning, cancer cells usually remain at their original site. The cancer is said to be localized. Later, cancer cells may metastasize, or invade neighboring organs or tissue. This occurs either by direct extension, or growth of the cancer, or by cancer cells detaching and being carried through the lymph or blood systems to other parts of the body. Metastasis may be regional—that is, confined to one region of the body. If left untreated, however, cancer is likely to spread. Such advanced cancers usually result in death.

Wright's weapon against cancer was chemotherapy, the medical use of chemicals. Because they grow more rapidly than most normal cells, cancer cells are especially sensitive to certain chemicals. The rapid growth of cancer cells means that they have greater needs than the normal cells of the body. Certain chemicals can interfere with these needs and possibly stop the abnormal growth.

In the early 1950s, when Wright began her campaign against cancer, the idea of fighting cancer with chemicals was still an experimental one. Cancer chemotherapy had its beginnings on a battlefield in France during the First World War. A number of American infantrymen had been gassed by the Germans. In the field hospital, it was discovered that the gas had damaged the bodily system that makes white blood cells.

Since the overproduction of white blood cells is the most common feature of blood cancer (leukemia), the gas seemed to be a way to treat leukemia. The gas was mustard gas. By 1946, scientists had developed a liquid called nitrogen mustard, which slowed down the overproduction of white blood cells in leukemia victims. Later research proved nitrogen mustard effective against other cancers as well.

Nitrogen mustard is an alkylating chemical—it adds chemical groups to certain substances in the cell, thus disrupting cell division and, in turn, growth of the cancer. Dr. Wright began her career as a cancer researcher by studying another chemical called triethylene melamine (TEM), also thought to be an effective alkylating agent against cancer.

TEM had been proven effective against leukemia in mice. Dr. Wright decided to try it against certain human leukemias and cancers of the lymphatic system, such as Hodgkin's disease.

She had a patient take one dose of TEM every day for a week. This was followed by one dose a week for five more weeks. Within two weeks, 10 out of 11 victims of Hodgkin's disease began to feel better. The painful swollen glands in the neck shrank, and the abdominal pains ceased. For some patients, TEM halted the disease for five years before they needed more treatment. Further testing showed TEM to be equally effective against four other types of cancer similar to Hodgkin's.

But neither nitrogen mustard nor TEM was effective against severe leukemia or many other kinds of cancer. Dr. Wright decided to test a new group of chemicals called antimetabolites. Such chemicals block the production of important components of the cancer cell's nucleus.

From the wards of Harlem Hospital, Wright selected 93 cancer patients. Surgery and radiation therapy had failed to cure their cancer. Wright started the patients on doses of different antimetabolites. Of the 93 cases, 54 showed improvement of some kind. Though they were helped for a while, most of these patients later died of cancer. But the chemicals had prolonged their lives.

There seemed to be a bright future for chemotherapy, and for Jane Wright as well. In 1955, Dr. Wright accepted a new job at New York University Medical Center, where she began to explore that promise.

The Cure in a Test Tube

Dr. Wright began looking for ways to perfect the use of chemicals. She knew that there were at least 20 or 30 anti-cancer chemicals. But which ones worked best for which cancers? There should be a better way to determine this than by giving different chemicals to patients and watching for the disappearance of the cancer, she thought.

Dr. Wright developed an intriguing approach to this problem. Why not let the cancer cells themselves tell the story? She would study changes in the cancer cells as the chemical did its work. She would then have a test-tube method of predicting the effects of different drugs on the more than 100 known types of cancers.

A tiny bit of the patient's tumor would be removed at surgery and placed in a flask of protein-rich fluid. By carefully regulating the temperature and the chemicals in the flask, Dr. Wright would grow the tumor cells in what is called a tissue culture. Then, the anti-cancer chemical to be tested would be added to the flask of cells. At the same time, the patient would be started on doses of the same chemical. Microscopic views of the cells in the flasks would be compared with the condition of the patient. Thus, Dr. Wright would get a microscopic view of what was happening to the cancer.

For example, one patient with Hodgkin's disease had painfully swollen lymph nodes in his neck. A tiny bit of one of those nodes was removed and grown in a tissue culture. TEM, the alkylating chemical, was added to the tissue culture. At the same time, the man was started on doses of TEM. After several weeks of TEM therapy, the nodes in the man's neck began to shrink. A check of the cells in the tissue culture showed wholesale destruction of the cancer cells.

Now, Wright had a tool for studying the chemotherapy of cancer. Once she knew the kind of cell changes to look for in each kind of tumor, Dr. Wright could then use a tissue culture of cancer cells to determine which chemical to use in treatment. In the case of Hodgkin's, for example, cell destruction seemed to be the thing to look for when testing an anti-cancer chemical.

Dr. Wright also found that tissue cultures were an excellent way to find out how a new chemical stopped the growth of cancer. When a new anti-cancer chemical made from the periwinkle plant became available, Dr. Wright tested it in tissue culture.

Studying the cancer cells after they had been exposed to the chemical, Dr. Wright discovered that most of the cells had simply stopped in an early stage of division. Dr. Wright's theory was that the new chemical interfered with cell division by blocking the role of the cell's cytoplasm. From that experiment, Dr. Wright went on to laboratory testing of other cancers and other chemicals.

Now, when a new cancer victim was admitted to the hospital, Dr. Wright could consult the charts produced through her research to find the best chemical to give the patient. Just to be sure, she would first expose a tissue culture of the patient's cancer cells to the chemical.

Dr. Wright also turned her attention to better ways of getting the chemical to the cancer cells. From her work with tissue cultures, Wright had decided that giving the chemical by mouth or injection was not always the most effective way of delivering the chemical to the cancer cells deep inside the body.

The chemical might have to travel quite a distance and through many parts of the body before it reached the cancerous area. By then, some of the chemical might have been picked up by other parts of the body.

Other scientists had developed a technique called perfusion. This involved injecting the chemical into the major blood vessel supplying the cancer. It was often used as a kind of "mopping-up" operation of stray cancer cells following the surgical removal of a tumor.

But now Wright could see other uses for perfusion. Perfusion could be a simple way to deliver the chemical directly to the tumor. And there were other advantages, too. Most chemicals produced side effects in patients since they attacked any cell in a stage of rapid growth. Typical side effects were nausea and a lowering of resistance to infection. But if the chemical could be routed directly to the tumor, then side effects could certainly be reduced, if not avoided altogether.

The perfusion technique also seemed an excellent way of treating patients who had a cancer that could not be removed by surgeons because of its location or extensive spread. And perfusion could be the answer for patients facing the amputation of a cancerous limb.

Dr. Wright began testing perfusion as a way of giving chemotherapy to cancer patients. She tested 52 patients, with cancers of the head, neck, ovary, and other areas. The perfusion technique involved locating the major artery and vein serving the cancerous area.

Using a special needle, the artery and vein were connected, creating a kind of circulatory detour. Tourniquets were used to prevent the chemical from leaking out of this detour into the rest of the body. Then, the chemical was pumped into the needle connecting the two blood vessels.

Dr. Wright found that perfusion seemed to work best on tumors of the head, limbs, and pelvis. Studying some of the cancers after perfusion, she noted that, first, the tumor grew dark and dry. Then, it started to break up and shrink. Of the 52 patients she studied, 32 were helped by the procedure. But no tumor disappeared completely.

It has been a long road—this chemical search for a cancer cure—and still no cure has been found. But Dr. Wright has seen cancer slowed by chemicals. One success she is very proud of is her battle against a fatal form of skin cancer, a disease that surgery and radiation cannot help and that often produces horrible disfigurement of the person's face. One man treated by Dr. Wright had the disease over his entire body, except for his hands, feet, and scalp. Big, bluish red lumps had twisted his face out of shape. But after 30 days of treatment with chemicals, his face was completely clear, with only a few whitish scars where the lumps had been. His disease flared up several times. But each time it was stopped by chemotherapy.

Out of the Laboratory

The world of laboratories and hospitals is not the only place where Dr. Wright has waged a battle against cancer. In 1963, Wright served on President Lyndon Johnson's Commission on Heart Disease, Cancer, and Stroke. After many meetings, the commission came to the conclusion that better use of medical research was needed.

The commission recommended that disease centers be located in different parts of the country. In the centers, everything that is known about diagnosing and treating heart disease, cancer, and stroke would be put into action.

In July 1967, Wright was appointed an associate dean and professor of surgery at New York Medical College. Her position as a dean was the highest post ever attained by an African-American woman in medical administration. Along with her administrative duties, Dr. Wright continued her cancer research and worked on research programs for heart disease and stroke.

Jane Wright was also responsible for educating other doctors about chemotherapy. She pointed out that with the current state of knowledge about cancer, 50 percent of the people who develop cancer could be cured. Wright was critical of the amount of money available for cancer research. Some $170 million in federal government money was spent on cancer research a year, while $358 million was spent in the United States for chewing gum and $553 million on greeting cards in a year.

"If we can afford these things," Jane Wright asked, "why can't we put enough money to work to solve the cancer problem?"

Dr. Wright has been one of the most vigorous and creative of the group of medical scientists who are engaged in the attack on cancer. Her goal has been to discover more effective chemical treatment by using tissue cultures from individual patients, rather than from laboratory mice or other animals, to predict the effects of drugs.

This idea was a pioneering contribution to the treatment of cancer. Dr. Jane Wright worked on every type of cancer, from skin cancer to breast cancer, from Hodgkin's to leukemia. She is credited with being the first doctor to gain remissions in patients with mycosis fungoides, a type of skin cancer, and in solid breast cancer tumors.

In 1971, Jane Wright was the first woman elected as president of the New York Cancer Society. As one of the seven founding members of the American Society of Clinical Oncology, the pre-eminent organization in the field of cancer research, Dr. Jane Wright extended her leadership role in cancer research.

As a member of the National Medical Association, the American Association for Cancer Research, the New York Academy of Sciences, the American Medical Association, and the African Medical and Research Foundation, her influence in American medicine has been extensive.

In 1961, Dr. Wright was part of a medical group sponsored by the African Research Foundation that treated some 340 cancer patients in Kenya (East Africa) using a mobile medical unit. As she moved toward retirement in 1985, Dr. Wright led delegates to Ghana (West Africa), China, Eastern Europe, and the (former) Soviet Union to share and learn about the latest knowledge and techniques in cancer chemotherapy research and treatment.

Writing about her cancer research has always been an important part of Dr. Wright's professional work. She has authored or co-authored 135 published articles and nine chapters on cancer in medical textbooks.

Beginning in 1984, Jane Wright started a series of articles titled "Update in Cancer Chemotherapy" for the *Journal of the National Medical Association.* Her articles covered the latest information on breast cancer, lung cancer, gastrointestinal cancer, genitourinary cancer, ovarian cancer, skin cancer, and cancers of the bone, muscle, and nervous tissue.

Today, cancer remains a dreaded disease. It is still difficult to treat. The American Cancer Society, in its 1990 annual report, stated that "the incidence of cancer is increasing. Cancer is the disease which is the major health concern of Americans today." One out of every five deaths in the United States is from cancer. More than 500,000 people die each year from the disease.

In the early 1900s, few cancer patients had any hope of long-term survival. In the 1930s, only one in five cancer patients was alive five years after treatment. By the 1960s, however, that figure was one in three.

Today, about 440,000 Americans, or 40 percent of patients who get cancer, survive five years after treatment. Cancer is now treated by surgery, chemicals, radiation, radioactive substances, hormones, and immunotherapy. The use of combinations of cancer drugs has resulted in remarkably improved survival rates. The years of research by doctors like Jane Wright has led the way to the progress made in fighting cancer.

EUGENE W. ADAMS

8

There is really very little difference between animal medicine and human medicine. Diseases in animals and humans are similar. When an animal has pneumonia or cancer, the symptoms are the same as in people. And so are the changes in body organs and tissues. Infections in animals and people are the same kind of problem.

"While veterinary, or animal, medicine is concerned with the disease and health of animals, it plays an important role in human health because we live so close to many animals and depend on some for our food. A veterinarian, or animal doctor, is by profession perhaps the greatest humanitarian that one can think of—a very special kind of doctor. We are concerned with both animal life and its effect on human life at the same time."

This is how Eugene Adams, a veterinarian, describes his profession. Dr. Adams has been a veterinarian for more than 45 years. In the world of animal medicine, he has been a meat inspector, teacher, researcher, a designer of veterinary programs in Africa, and a pioneer builder of the School of Veterinary Medicine at Tuskegee University in Tuskegee, Alabama.

"I had ideas of becoming a dentist when I entered Wichita High School in Wichita, Kansas. But one evening changed all that," observed Dr. Adams. "I was attending a father-and-son banquet at the Wichita YMCA. Sitting at a table next to my father and me was a black man, Dr. Thomas G. Perry. He didn't have any children of his own, but he was there that evening with another young boy whose father had passed away. Dr. Perry was this boy's father for the evening, and this really impressed me and drew my attention to him."

Dr. Adams continued: "As I sat there listening to the various speakers, I began to think about what Dr. Perry did to make a living. He was a veterinarian and the owner of one of the first animal hospitals in Wichita and the entire Midwest in the 1920s."

When the banquet was over, young Gene Adams met Dr. Perry. "Could I visit your animal hospital?" he asked.

"Of course," replied Dr. Perry, never imagining that Adams would one day enter the field of animal medicine.

Gene knew another black man who was working in public health in Wichita. This man was a meat inspector at a local meat packing plant. He prepared slaughtered animals for inspection by veterinarians at the plant.

"Between my junior and senior years in high school, I needed to earn some money and was able to land a job at the meat plant. And so I learned that caring for dogs and cats wasn't the only kind of work for a veterinarian."

During his senior year, Gene Adams spent time at Dr. Perry's animal hospital. Dr. Perry had graduated from the School of Veterinary Medicine at Kansas State University in 1926. He had become one of the first veterinarians to have a successful small-animal practice in this country. He was a specialist in the treatment of greyhound racing dogs. Perry's work in the field of veterinary medicine for small animals was widely known in the Midwest during the almost three decades of his practice.

Because of his respect for Perry, Gene Adams decided on a career in veterinary medicine instead of dentistry. He went to Kansas State University after high school, and after two years of college study, he was ready to apply for admission to the School of Veterinary Medicine.

Dr. Perry feared that Adams wouldn't be accepted to veterinary school because of his race, but Gene Adams had studied hard in high school and college. His grades were good, and he was accepted. In 1944, he graduated with his doctor's degree in veterinary medicine.

"What Are the Qualifications?"

In 1944, World War II was raging on the battlefields of Europe. Dr. Adams wanted to return to Wichita to work with Dr. Perry, but he was eligible to be drafted into the Army. His draft board informed him that working at a small-animal medical practice wasn't considered essential to the country's war effort, and Gene Adams found himself a member of the U.S. Army.

White graduates of veterinary schools were drafted into the Army as first lieutenants. However, the situation was different for graduates who were African Americans. When Dr. Adams and another black veterinarian arrived at Fort Riley Army Base, they were told that they would have to enter as privates.

Gene Adams refused to accept such discriminatory treatment. He decided to work for the government as a civilian and was assigned to the Meat Inspection Service of the Department of Agriculture in St. Louis, Missouri. The job of a meat inspector was considered essential to the country's war effort.

Meat inspectors examine animal organs for traces of disease. Meat from diseased animals can be dangerous to humans. Dr. Adams examined more than 7,000 hogs, 400 cattle, and 300 sheep each day.

"I had only three assistants, so I saw a lot of animals," Adams recalled.

After two years as a meat inspector, Dr. Adams felt that he was clearly qualified to become a supervisor at the slaughterhouse. "Gene, you're as big as you're going to get here," replied the inspector in charge when Dr. Adams asked about a promotion.

"What are the qualifications for becoming a supervisor?" Adams wanted to know.

"Well, one of them is to be white," was the reply.

Dr. Adams decided to move.

In 1947, there was an outbreak of hoof-and-mouth disease in Mexico. The problem was so bad that American veterinarians were being sent to Mexico in large numbers, and Adams thought it would be a good chance for him to leave St. Louis. Again, he went to his supervisor.

"Well, Gene, the only way you could go to Mexico would be for me to declare you surplus," the supervisor said, "and I'd lose a good man. I can't do that."

That was the last time Dr. Adams went to him for a new assignment.

Dr. Adams' seven years as a meat inspector did bring a lasting reward. They developed his interest and background in diseases in animals and animal organs, such as the liver, kidneys, and brain. He went on to become an outstanding researcher, teacher, and leader in the field of animal pathology, the study of the cause and treatment of diseases.

"The Best Decision I Have Ever Made"

Tuskegee University in southern Alabama is a black college founded by Booker T. Washington in 1881. It was to Tuskegee that George Washington Carver had come in

1896. There, Carver's research with plants revolutionized southern agricultural practices and improved the health and economy of the entire country. In 1944, Dr. Perry had left Kansas to help start a school of veterinary medicine at Tuskegee, and it was at Tuskegee that Dr. Adams was to find his professional roots.

In 1950, Adams received an offer to come to Tuskegee to teach. His days as a meat inspector were finally over. "Coming to Tuskegee was the best decision I have ever made in my life," Dr. Adams said. "It gave me the opportunity to advance educationally and to become involved in so many interesting things."

During the next 25 years, Gene Adams played a major role in building Tuskegee's School of Veterinary Medicine into one of the leading schools of its kind in the country and world.

From 1951 to 1956, Gene Adams was an instructor and, later, an assistant professor in the Department of Pathology and Parasitology at the school. When he arrived at Tuskegee, there were few teaching materials in the field of pathology.

Not only did Dr. Adams have to prepare animal tissue sections, but, as he remarked, "I had to learn how to teach pathology to students. I soon realized that to advance as a teacher of animal pathology, one has to be on the frontiers of new knowledge through scientific research and further training."

In 1956, Dr. Adams left Tuskegee to attend Cornell University for a year. There, he worked and studied as a researcher in pathology and microbiology. In June 1957, he returned to Tuskegee with a master of science degree in comparative pathology. He was promoted to the rank of associate professor.

In addition to becoming a skilled medical research scientist, Dr. Adams had gained some new ideas about teaching pathology. "I came back to Tuskegee knowing that pathology must be taught by actually studying disease in real situations—that is, with sick animals brought to a clinic for treatment. We had to begin teaching veterinary students how to relate symptoms of a disease to body organ changes, to blood and urine analysis, and tissue examination under a microscope."

Decoding the "Message"

Dr. Adams developed a unique case history approach to learning about animal disease. He told his students that every dead animal has a "message" for us: "An animal becomes sick or dies because of a series of things that happened in the animal's body; in pathology, the changes in the animal body must be traced carefully to seek and understand the cause of death and illness."

To improve his teaching further, Dr. Adams returned to Cornell University in 1959. One of his professors was doing research on leukemia, a type of cancer that affects blood, in cats. This research sparked Dr. Adams' interest in studying cancer.

As described in the chapter on Dr. Jane Wright (see Chapter 7), cancer is a disease in which some cells in the body begin to produce more and more cells of the same kind in an uncontrolled fashion. The result is a mass of cells, or a tumor, that can damage the tissue (such as the brain, lungs, or bone) in which it has grown.

Often, cancer cells spread from one part of the body to another, causing damage to healthy, normal body cells and tissues. Cancer is the second leading killer of human beings, yet no one knows its exact cause. It can occur in almost any part of the body—the brain, skin, liver, lungs, bone, or blood.

The research work of veterinarians like Dr. Adams can lead to important discoveries in the cause and treatment of similar diseases in humans. Research in animal diseases usually comes before research involving humans. Dr. Adams devoted more than 15 years to studying cancer in dogs.

Adams explained the importance of his work this way: "The dog is a good animal model of man. Both are meat eaters, and dogs live close to man—that is, in the same environment. So perhaps what we learn about cancer in dogs may help us to understand cancer in humans."

What is it that causes normal body cells to "run wild" and begin producing a tumor?

Adams studied a tumor in dogs that is transmissible. (This means that if cells are taken from a tumor growing in one dog and injected into a healthy dog, the second dog will develop the same kind of tumor.) He discovered that a dog that has survived the growth and surgical removal of a tumor will be immune to new growths. The dog will not grow tumors when injected with the same kind of cancerous cells as before.

Dr. Adams has been able to cultivate, or grow, dog tumor cells outside of a dog's body, in a test tube, in what is called a tissue culture. He has kept the cells alive in an artificial environment for months at a time. This allows him to study the cancer cell's multiplication activity. It is an achievement that few other researchers have been able to manage.

In examining blood from dogs with cancer, Dr. Adams found changes in the amounts of certain proteins in their blood, especially those with tumors caused by cancer cells injected into a healthy dog. These blood protein changes are similar to protein changes caused by viral infections and other infectious diseases in humans and in domestic animals. This may mean that a virus causes tumor growth in dogs.

Dr. Adams' contributions to research and teaching have received national recognition. His cancer research has been commended by the National Cancer Institute and the U.S. Public Health Service. In 1964, he was the first African American elected to the American College of Veterinary Pathologists.

During the same year, Dr. Adams received the Norden Award for Distinguished Teaching in the Field of Veterinary Medicine. And when Kansas State University, his alma mater, received a grant from the U.S. government to set up a school of veterinary medicine in Africa, Dr. Adams was asked to head the project.

147

Different Continents, Different Problems

In June 1970, Dr. Eugene Adams arrived at Ahmadu Bello University in Zaria (in the north-central region of the African country of Nigeria). "When I arrived in Nigeria, I saw a chance to repeat some of the same things I had done at Tuskegee in my earlier years there," Dr. Adams later recalled.

"Although my job was to develop and teach animal disease and public health courses," he continued, "there were no teaching materials at hand. The Nigerians also needed applied research. So I could see myself starting out as I had 20 years earlier."

Dr. Adams began to develop a program that combined research and teaching. The research had to be related to the problems in Nigeria, not the problems faced in the United States. In fact, the Nigerian vets had been trained at Tuskegee. They knew little about the tropical animal diseases of Africa.

Animals and humans live closely together in Africa. Goats, chickens, and ducks share the same quarters as humans. Since tuberculosis is common in cattle, its transfer to humans is a danger in Africa.

One of Dr. Adams' first tasks was to document the diseases that were rampant in animals living close to the Nigerians—cattle, horses, poultry, sheep, and goats.

Since the Nigerians had no program to diagnose such diseases, there could be no treatment until Dr. Adams helped to design a center where animal blood and feces could be checked for bacteria and parasites. An animal-treatment clinic was put "on wheels" and moved out to the rural areas so that people could bring their animals for diagnosis and treatment.

Dr. Adams' training as a meat inspector was helpful in the area of public health. He set up a slaughterhouse with an inspection program for animals that were to be sold as meat. Parasites and worms that cause disease and infections were commonly found in the livestock.

Dr. Adams returned from Africa to Tuskegee University in 1972. He left behind programs to control diseases that could be passed from animals to people. And he had taught improved methods of raising livestock to increase the protein food supply necessary for human health.

The Tuskegee Program

His return to Tuskegee marked the beginning of an important phase of Adams' work in veterinary medicine. Upon his return, he was promoted to associate dean of the School of Veterinary Medicine and full professor of veterinary medicine. As associate dean, he had new and different responsibilities. He could no longer devote time to teaching. To many students, this was a disappointment.

One of those students, Dr. Leon Cruise, wrote to Dr. Adams when he learned that his former teacher was not going to be in the classroom:

> Ten years have passed since I graduated from Tuskegee. These years have taught me to appreciate the teaching that you provided to me and those in my class. . . .

I was somewhat saddened and disappointed to learn that you were no longer available to students as a teacher, . . . that you have moved out of the classroom and into an administrative position at the school.

Dr. Adams responded to his former student:

My decision to move most of my time to administration was not an easy one. Perhaps the one event that helped me most to make this decision was a statement made by the head of the Department of Clinical Medicine, School of Veterinary Medicine, at Cambridge, England. The essence of his statement was that only those of us who participate actively in both *research* and *teaching* can appreciate the complex problems of making the total educational program successful. A major concern of mine is to participate in the development of a strong program in teaching and research here at Tuskegee.

The School of Veterinary Medicine at Tuskegee was established in 1945. At that time, there were no other schools in the South where African Americans could study veterinary medicine. When Dr. Adams came to Tuskegee in 1950, the veterinary medicine program was still in its infancy, the first graduates having received their degrees in 1949.

According to Dr. Adams, "Unless more veterinarians can be trained, the nation will be faced with a shortage of more than 10,000 veterinarians by the year 2000." The educational resources to do the necessary training are the 25 schools of veterinary medicine in the United States.

Tuskegee's School of Veterinary Medicine is the only veterinary school in the United States that is located at a predominantly black college. It is in a unique position to supply the United States with the veterinary workers that it needs. In a way that no other school can, Tuskegee can provide an opportunity for blacks to enter the health professions through the field of veterinary medicine.

Of the more than 46,000 veterinarians in the United States, only 940 are black. Many of them studied animal pathology under Dr. Adams and received their training from a program that he spent 25 years helping to build. Tuskegee University has served as a national resource in preparing more than 70 percent of the black veterinarians in this country.

The program at Tuskegee, a private university, has been developed with great difficulty. It has not received the same level of financial support given to many other schools, especially those institutions that are run by the larger state universities.

Although the school's original purpose was to provide an opportunity for black students in the South to study veterinary medicine, the program, along with others at Tuskegee, is open to all students without regard to race, religion, or national background.

"We are not operating a black veterinary school, but one that happens to be black," says Dr. Adams.

The training of vets from outside the United States has also been an important part of Tuskegee's program. Students come from such countries as Canada, Jamaica, Haiti, Nigeria, Ethiopia, and Puerto Rico. When Dr. Adams arrived in Nigeria in 1970 to teach, he found 16 of his former students working as veterinarians.

Though most veterinarians are employed at private animal hospitals, there is a wide variety of opportunities in the field of animal medicine. Working for government agencies that provide public health services is one career choice for veterinarians. (More than 2,000 veterinarians work for the U.S. Department of Agriculture.)

Teaching and basic medical research are the roles that Dr. Adams chose. Aerospace medicine, radiological health, livestock production, animal health management, and environmental health and safety are other areas of work for veterinarians. The U.S. Public Health Service, the U.S. Food and Drug Administration, and the World Health Organization all employ veterinarians. Many commercial firms use animals—and thus veterinary skills—in producing and testing medicines.

In 1983, a new position for Dr. Adams at Tuskegee greatly increased his influence on world health problems. Tuskegee's president, Benjamin F. Payton, appointed him as vice provost for international programs.

Tuskegee's international programs provided technical assistance in agricultural science, animal health care, and health education in Haiti and Jamaica as well as in the African countries of Liberia, Senegal, Nigeria, Tanzania, Ghana, Mali, and Swaziland. As vice provost, Dr. Adams' new responsibilities also included overseeing the progress of some 150 students from 50 foreign countries who were studying at Tuskegee.

After more than 38 years of service as a teacher, a researcher, and a college administrator, Dr. Eugene Adams retired from Tuskegee University in May 1989. Dr. Adams' lifelong dedication to understanding and treating animal and related human health problems makes up an important chapter in medical history. Dr. Eugene Adams was a leader in veterinary science.

In retirement, Eugene Adams continues to work on health projects such as waste management and alternative agriculture. But Adams' special project is one that only he could undertake—writing the history of the School of Veterinary Medicine at Tuskegee University.

ANGELLA D. FERGUSON

9

The tiny African-American baby girl had just been admitted to the hospital. Her hands and feet were painfully swollen. She lay in her hospital crib, first sobbing, then whimpering. Her swollen hands lay stiffly outstretched on the sheets. The child's mother hovered over the bed, helplessly watching her baby suffer while the doctors tried to find out what was wrong.

The diagnosis was not slow in coming: sickle cell anemia. The baby had inherited the incurable disease from her parents, just as she had inherited her brown skin. The mother's sorrow doubled. Not only was her baby very sick, but she and the baby's father had unwittingly given their baby the sickness.

Pain, suffering, and sorrowful, guilt-ridden parents—these are Dr. Angella Ferguson's first memories of sickle cell anemia, the disease that she studied for nearly 20 years of her life. Ferguson was a young intern when she saw her first case of sickle cell anemia.

As a medical student, she had learned that sickle cell anemia is a disease that mainly afflicts black people. It was brought to the United States in the genes of enslaved Africans. The disease stems from a defect in the chemical structure of hemoglobin, the oxygen-carrying substance that gives blood its color. Such flawed hemoglobin is called hemoglobin-S.

When the body needs more oxygen than normal—when it is infected or fatigued, for instance—hemoglobin-S forms crystal-like rods in the blood cells. When this happens, normally donut-shaped red blood cells are distorted into sickle-like shaped cells. The misshapen blood cells clog the blood vessels. The disruption of the normal flow of life-giving blood results in pain, swelling, and damage to other organs in the body.

People who have sickle cell anemia have inherited the gene for hemoglobin-S from both parents. A person who inherits a hemoglobin-S gene from only one parent is said to have a sickle cell trait. A person with a sickle cell trait has a few of the red blood cells that carry hemoglobin-S, but he or she seldom has any problems. Such people may live most of their lives with no knowledge of the genetic trait they carry.

Dr. Ferguson had learned this much about sickle cell anemia in medical school. She was to add much more information to that body of knowledge.

What Is Normal?

Dr. Angella Ferguson chose a career in pediatrics, the branch of medicine that deals with the care of infants and children, at the end of a long search.

Born and raised in Washington, D.C., Ferguson had enrolled in the business program at Cardoza High School. She planned to become a secretary and then an accountant. She even worked briefly as a secretary for the U.S. Navy in Washington.

But her father urged her to go on to college, so Angella took some college prep courses in her senior year. As a sophomore at Howard University, Angella took a chemistry course. She found it more interesting than shorthand. She also studied biology and anatomy. Excited by these new interests, Ferguson pursued her studies and graduated from Howard University Medical School in 1949.

As a medical graduate, Ferguson donned a white coat and began working in the wards of Freedmen's Hospital in Washington, D.C. She found herself increasingly drawn to the sick children. She felt a need to help them.

Following her internship, Dr. Ferguson completed a two-year training program in pediatrics before starting a private practice as a pediatrician. But as she began seeing her first patients, she felt the need for more knowledge about black babies.

When a mother asked "How soon should my baby crawl?" or "When will she cut a tooth?" Dr. Ferguson was not certain of the answer. She knew that most growth and developmental standards for children were determined by studying white babies. She wasn't sure that such standards fit black babies.

Ferguson found this lack of knowledge troubling, for only by being certain of what is normal can a pediatrician detect abnormally developing babies. So she decided to find out for herself what the normal development of black babies was really like.

Dr. Ferguson put aside her private practice and joined forces with another Washington pediatrician, Dr. Roland Scott. Together, they launched a study of the growth and developmental patterns of black babies.

Their plan was to travel about the country to various hospitals and clinics and study healthy black babies. They used two basic survey techniques—cross sectional and longitudinal. In a cross-sectional study, the doctors would gather certain information about many babies of exactly the same age. In a longitudinal study, they would observe an individual child for a certain period of time.

It was in the well-baby clinics that the researchers made their most significant discovery. A well-baby clinic provides health care for newborn babies. The babies are brought in at regular intervals for immunizations (shots) and physical exams. Thus, Dr. Ferguson was able to follow a healthy child for a year or more. She found that many black babies learned to sit up, pull up, and walk earlier than many white babies. Why was this?

The answer seemed more related to the environment than to the racial background of the baby. Babies born into poor families did not have playpens or highchairs. They were not restrained from moving about on their own as they wished. The children were propped up more and learned to sit sooner. Thus, a study that started out to provide better answers about black babies also seemed to provide clues about the healthy development of all babies.

Suffering Children

But as Angella Ferguson studied normal babies, the sight of certain other babies in the clinics and hospitals haunted her. These were the tiny victims of sickle cell anemia. She began to direct her research activities toward helping these suffering children.

Dr. Ferguson had assigned herself a difficult task. She knew that sickle cell anemia was inherited, so there could be no immediate hope of prevention. The only approach, it seemed, was to study the painful symptoms and find ways to relieve them.

For the sickle cell victim, the most dangerous and painful time is called the crisis. Sickle cell crises can strike at any time and in any part of the body. During such a crisis, the logjam of sickled cells cuts off the flow of blood through blood vessels, triggering such symptoms as pain and swelling due to the blocking up of body fluids. Other symptoms, such as skin ulcers and brain damage, may be the result of tissue dying for lack of nourishing blood. Thus, sickle cell crises can mimic other sicknesses such as heart attack, pneumonia, and even strokes.

Sorting Out the Symptoms

Sorting through the symptoms, Dr. Ferguson and her research team managed to classify the symptoms by age groups. They found that from birth to two years, most sickle cell victims suffered arthritic-like symptoms of pain and swelling in the joints, especially the ankles and wrists.

From age two to six, abdominal pains were the most frequent symptoms. These pains were due to the swelling of internal organs, such as the liver and spleen, which also caused the child to develop a potbelly.

From age 6 to 12, the symptoms grew milder. But at age 12, as the child's body began to mature, the disease often flared up again. It was then that the sickle cell victim often developed ulcers on the legs.

These symptoms, however, did not always provide a reliable guide for detecting a victim. One tragic case that Dr. Ferguson treated was that of a six-year-old boy who seemed perfectly well until he had his tonsils removed. The anesthesia used during the operation brought on a sickle cell crisis that affected his brain. The boy was unconscious and paralyzed for several days. Then, slowly, he regained consciousness and the use of his body. But over the next 18 months, he had four more brain crises. Finally, he died. The autopsy showed a brain that was almost completely destroyed by the disease. Yet the boy had not shown the slightest sign of having sickle cell anemia until his tonsils were removed.

Even out of this tragedy, medical researchers learned something new about sickle cell anemia. They learned that the sickle cell victim must be given a great deal of oxygen after surgery in order to prevent a crisis.

Avoiding the Crisis

Now having tracked down the symptoms of sickle cell anemia, Dr. Ferguson turned her attention to the cause of the crisis itself. A diary kept on each patient provided a day-by-day account of the health happenings in each child's life. Then, when a sickle cell crisis developed, Dr. Ferguson simply consulted the diary for clues as to what might have brought on the attack. Quite often the cause was an infection.

Laboratory tests on the children revealed two other important clues. The blood of the sickle cell victim in crisis was thicker and often more acidic than it should have been. Using this information as a guide, Dr. Ferguson set about finding ways to prevent sickle cell crisis.

She began by attacking the problem of thick blood. Giving fluids through a needle in the vein thinned out the blood. But Ferguson found that simply having the child drink large amounts of water achieved the same effect. She enlisted the parents in the water project. They were advised to keep a jug of water in the refrigerator for the child. Dr. Ferguson would say to the mother, "Tell your child, 'Drink that jug empty.' "

Since drinking so much water could produce another problem, teachers were requested to let the child go to the bathroom as often as necessary. Dr. Ferguson also learned that adding small amounts of bicarbonate, an alkaline substance, to the drinking water seemed to adjust the acidity of the blood.

Sickle cell patients were put on a program of infection prevention. Children were kept away from people suffering from even minor infections. Colds were attacked head-on with nose drops and other medicines. A balanced diet and vitamins built up the children's resistance to infection. Personal hygiene problems, such as dental work, were taken care of when the child was feeling well.

"The Whole Child"

Out of this beginning grew a guide for treating the child. "We treat the whole child: the student, the family member, as well as the child in crisis," said Dr. Ferguson.

One problem troubling the child in school was the common belief that sickle cell victims were retarded, or slow to learn. A series of tests convinced Dr. Ferguson that such children had normal intelligence. She found that at times their appearance made them seem retarded.

Since the bony structure of the head is affected by the disease, these children might have a slight point to their heads. And because their organs were often swollen, they might have extended abdomens. They were often very short. Their fingernails and the whites of their eyes were sometimes yellow. But Dr. Ferguson traced most learning problems the children seemed to be having to their frequent absenteeism from school due to their crisis periods and health problems. She recommended the use of tutors for children who missed school and asked teachers to give such children special attention.

Dr. Ferguson also found that the parents of the sickle cell victim needed attention. They often felt guilty when they found the child had inherited the disease from them. The guilt, the financial strain, the care of a frequently sick child—these factors took their toll on the parents.

Sometimes, parents responded to the illness by denying the child affection. More often, they spoiled the child, and this produced problems among the other children in the family.

It helped to give the parents psychological counseling. Often, just explaining why they shouldn't feel guilty for passing on the disease to the child was enough.

But the parents were always made to understand that they were an important part of the health team treating the child.

Trying New Treatments

During the time that Dr. Ferguson was devoting her attention to the symptoms and treatment of sickle cell anemia, other scientists were studying ways to change the shape of the sickled red cell. Many chemicals, such as urea and cyanate compounds, were tried.

As Dr. Ferguson learned of these new ideas, she tried them on her patients. Some worked; some did not. But most were dangerous chemicals—too dangerous, she felt—to give a child for any length of time.

Then, in the late 1960s, sickle cell anemia began to get a great deal of publicity. Many scientists, some of them eager to get research funds, were trying all sorts of new treatments. After years of study of the disease, Ferguson knew that many of the ideas then being proposed simply wouldn't work.

For example, some scientists wanted to experiment with exchange blood transfusions, a process in which the patient's blood would be removed and replaced with that of a normal person. Dr. Ferguson knew that the patient's body would replace the normal blood cells with sickled ones. Exchange transfusion was a painful and temporary solution at best.

Some businesses even started to use the disease as an advertising gimmick, offering to donate money to sickle cell research if people would buy their products. To Dr. Ferguson, it seemed that such publicity did little to help the victims of this disease. She felt that future research should be aimed at changing the genes in the victims' cells so that their bodies would no longer produce abnormal hemoglobin-S.

Before such a thing would be possible, much more needed to be learned about the responsible gene. Feeling that she had done all she could in sickle cell research, Dr. Ferguson moved on to new interests.

A New Challenge

For a while, it seemed that Angella Ferguson would go back to teaching and private practice. But that was not to be.

A new hospital was being planned for Howard University. Each medical department appointed a representative to outline the department's needs for the new hospital. "I made the presentation for pediatrics," said Dr. Ferguson.

The hospital planners were very impressed with her orderliness and logic in designing space for the delivery room and infant care. And so, quite unexpectedly, Howard University offered Dr. Ferguson the chance to do something different—to oversee the construction of the new Howard University hospital. She accepted the challenge and became director of programs and facilities.

The new hospital stood for something that was sorely needed by the black community of Washington, D.C. For the last 100 years, Freedmen's Hospital had borne the major burden of the health needs and medical education of Washington's black residents. The student doctors and nurses from Howard University had to crowd into the old structure to be trained in their professions. The hospital was built on the old "big ward" concept. Thirty patients shared each ward and one bathroom.

Finally, in the 1960s, the federal government decided to build a new hospital for Howard.

As Dr. Ferguson took on her new duties, she found that her major task was convincing the congressmen who controlled the budget for the new hospital that a teaching hospital had to be bigger than a community hospital.

Ferguson argued that more room was needed around a patient's bed so that medical students could learn from the physicians as they treated patients. More consulting rooms, where professors and doctors could talk to their students about patients, would be needed. Research labs and library rooms were needed. A fight was waged over the size of the kitchen area. Dr. Ferguson argued that test kitchens would be needed for dietetic interns.

"The Lady in the Hard Hat"

As the director of programs and facilities in the Office of Health Affairs, Dr. Ferguson became known as "the lady in the hard hat."

Every day, the lady in the hard hat could be seen moving through the construction site on the Howard campus, consulting with engineers and construction workers.

As Dr. Ferguson observed, it was quite a challenge: "I had to be totally familiar with the plans to be sure that patient care and health staffers would have appropriate space for the most efficient medical service delivery." She constantly reviewed the needs of the medical research and teaching programs to be certain that they were properly integrated into the physical space.

Ferguson kept the patients in mind, too. She insisted on semi-private rooms and an attractive environment—bright colors, carpets, piped-in music, even landscaping—for the patients to enjoy.

Dr. Ferguson's work on the hospital neared an end. She had pushed a $17 million budget to $43 million. But she had produced a modern teaching hospital—a facility that was more than twice as large as Freedmen's, one that was equipped with the most up-to-date medical facilities.

Finally, as the glass and stone building took shape and moving day approached, Dr. Ferguson found she had one more battle to fight. Neighborhood children found that the expensive parking lot lights made great targets. One night, just before Thanksgiving Day, they broke 30 of the lights, which cost $110 each.

Dr. Ferguson decided that these children needed to understand that the hospital was theirs. They were taken on a tour of the new building and given a Thanksgiving dinner. They were organized into the Courtesy Patrol and given orange jackets to wear.

The "Orange Jackets" began to serve the hospital by conducting tours, running elevators, and working at the reception desk. No more lights were broken. "Orange Jackets" were not even seen walking on the grass.

Patients were moved from the old Freedmen's Hospital to the new Howard University hospital in May 1975. The first baby was born in the new hospital 15 minutes after the move.

Vision and Energy

After the hospital was completed, Angella Ferguson was promoted to the position of associate vice president of health affairs. Her work as the developer of the physical environment for Howard's medical complex continued as she oversaw the construction of the new Seely G. Mudd Building of the College of Medicine (completed in 1979), new space in the College of Dentistry building (completed in 1982), and the Animal Research Center. Dr. Ferguson also headed the renovation of the College of Allied Health Science and the College of Nursing.

Dr. Ferguson's vision and energy did not stop with this new development work to her credit. In the late 1980s, she began the planning for a parking garage, a cancer research laboratory and patient care center, an adult day-care center, an ambulatory care area, new facilities for the Howard College of Pharmacy and College of Nursing, and staff quarters for doctors who needed to be nearby.

All of this expansion required more land around the hospital. Dr. Ferguson held many meetings with local civic and neighborhood groups to acquire new space on which to build. She faced great community resistance, but her negotiating skills enabled the neighborhood residents to see that the health service needs of the entire community would be better met.

After 42 years in medical care—half of those years in pediatrics and half in "bricks and mortar"—Dr. Ferguson retired in June 1991. She left to her community and her profession a legacy of important pediatric research and a vast medical complex.

More than 13,000 patients are admitted each year to the Howard University hospital. The emergency care area receives nearly 50,000 patient visits a year. The hospital prepares hundreds of health professionals each year. It brings critically needed services to the African-American community in the nation's capital.

And by no means least important, the hospital that Dr. Angella D. Ferguson worked so hard to build is home to some 1,500 births each year.

CHARLES R. DREW

10

Emergency! An ambulance races through the city streets. An automobile accident victim is rushed to a hospital. His body is bleeding from deep cuts. He is in shock. Blood—a lot of it—will be needed immediately.

At the hospital, a nurse phones the blood bank and orders blood plasma. Within minutes, several pints reach the emergency room. A doctor carefully pushes a needle into a vein in the victim's limp arm. A nurse connects a bottle of plasma to the needle with a plastic tube.

The plasma begins to flow into the vein. Three more pints are given. The lost blood is being replaced. Within a few hours, the victim's blood pressure begins to rise, and he comes out of shock. Another blood transfusion has helped to save a human life.

Every day in every part of the world, blood that once flowed in the blood vessels of a healthy person is put into the body of a sick or injured person. At this very moment, someone lying ill on a hospital bed is getting blood plasma taken from a donor weeks ago. This blood was preserved and stored in a blood bank until needed.

In the summer of 1940, a desperate plea for help came from across the Atlantic Ocean. Human blood was being spilled from the wounded bodies of men fighting in World War II. Soldiers in the battlefield and in hospitals lay close to death. Many of their lives were saved because fresh blood plasma from America was passed into the bodies of the injured men. Lives were saved because shipments of preserved plasma were flown to the foreign battlefields.

It was Charles R. Drew, an African-American medical doctor and scientist, who made possible the availability of stored blood plasma for blood transfusions. Dr. Drew did this by finding a way to preserve blood plasma for long periods of time.

Before Dr. Drew's work, there was no efficient way to store large quantities of blood for long periods of time. But when the wartime need for blood arose, Dr. Drew was ready. He had already set up a successful experimental blood bank to test his ideas about blood preservation.

Everyone has seen blood ooze from a cut finger. Most people can lose about a pint of blood before they begin to suffer any ill effects. If more blood is lost, though, there is a real health danger because the body cannot replace the lost blood fast enough.

Blood is made up of both a liquid portion and a solid portion. The two can be separated. If a sample of blood stands in a bottle, the solid part will settle to the bottom. The solid part consists of red blood cells and white blood cells. The liquid part of the blood will remain on top of the piled-up cells.

This liquid is called plasma. Plasma is mostly water, along with dissolved calcium, sodium, potassium, iron, copper, and other elements. Plasma also contains sugars, fats, and proteins. (These substances are dissolved in the plasma, too.)

In addition, plasma contains fibrinogen, a substance that makes blood clot; hormones, substances that control different body activities; and antibodies, substances that help the body fight disease-causing germs. For the body to function properly, the proportion of plasma in the blood must remain fairly constant.

Before Dr. Drew's time, the breakdown of red blood cells prevented the storing of blood for more than a day or two. When red blood cells broke down, the element potassium was released into the liquid part of the blood. This change spoiled the blood, and it had to be thrown away. Since it was very hard to get blood for transfusions, throwing it out was an unfortunate waste.

The Mysteries of Blood

It was the mysteries of blood that fascinated Charles Drew when he was a student in medical school. During the time he was studying and training to be a doctor, fresh whole blood—liquid and solid parts—was being used in blood transfusions. However, enough fresh whole blood was often not available. Charles Drew was not satisfied with the methods then being used to transfer blood from one person to another.

In August 1928, Drew arrived at McGill University (in Montreal, Canada) to study medicine. At this time, he was known primarily for his exceptional athletic ability. For two years before coming to McGill, Drew had been the director of athletics at Morgan State College in Baltimore, Maryland. At Morgan, Drew had produced fine teams in football and basketball.

Before his college coaching job, Drew himself was an outstanding college athlete. At his graduation ceremonies from Amherst College in Massachusetts, he was awarded a trophy as the athlete who had contributed the most to athletics during his four years at college. He had starred in football, basketball, baseball, and track, just as he had during his years (1918-1922) at Dunbar High School in Washington, D.C.

Even at McGill University, Drew's athletic achievements continued. He was elected captain of the track team and won Canadian championships in the high and low hurdles, the high jump, and the broad jump.

Charles Drew was a tough competitor. He might have become a professional athlete or coach, but his desire to become a doctor was stronger. His ability for scholarship and achievement in medical science more than kept pace with his athletic ability.

After five years of hard study and brilliant work, Drew graduated from medical school at the top of his class. He was awarded two degrees—one in medicine and one in surgery. Dr. Drew decided to remain in Montreal to continue his education and training in surgery. He became an intern and then a resident doctor at Montreal General Hospital. During this period, he continued to study and work 18 hours a day, as he had done as a medical student.

At Montreal General Hospital, an ongoing research program was to shape Dr. Drew's future. A laboratory had been set up for typing blood before transfusions. Four major blood types were known to medical scientists at the time. These were labeled A, B, AB, and O. A person's blood type depends on the presence of certain substances on the surface of red blood cells.

In general, a whole blood transfusion cannot be done unless the blood of the donor and the receiving patient are of the same type. (Type O blood, however, can be given to some recipients of other blood types.)

Using just any donor for a blood transfusion can be dangerous. If blood types are not matched properly, red blood cells will clump together and block the flow of blood in the blood vessels. The clumping of red blood cells can cause serious illness and even death.

Dr. John Beattie, one of Charles Drew's instructors in medical school, was doing research on blood in the new blood-typing laboratory. The two doctors had become close friends during Drew's student days. Drew had spent many hours in Dr. Beattie's lab, assisting his former teacher. Dr. Beattie introduced Drew to the excitement and challenge of scientific research.

Although the blood types A, B, AB, and O had been discovered in the year 1900, medical scientists were just beginning to learn about their meaning. There were still many mysteries. Dr. Drew began to read every book and article he could find on blood research.

As a young doctor working in the hospital's surgery division, Charles Drew had seen seriously ill and injured patients die from the loss of blood. He felt certain that some of them would have lived if blood could have been given quickly enough to restore the loss. He could not accept the fact that a patient lying on the operating room table might die because blood of the right type was not readily available.

Whenever blood transfusions were necessary, donors with a blood type that matched the patient's had to be found. The laboratory was often in turmoil. Technicians rushed madly to type the blood of the prospective donor and receiver. Hours would pass before the blood was ready for transfusion. The time lapse could mean the difference between life and death. Often, no blood donor of the right type was available. In one emergency, Dr. Drew gave blood from his own body for a man on the operating room table.

By 1935, Dr. Charles Drew had completed his medical residency in surgery at Montreal General. He was headed home to Washington, D.C. On his mind weighed a very bothersome problem.

Charles Drew kept asking himself how blood could be collected, preserved, and stored for medical emergencies. The delays and deaths that occurred before blood transfusions could be performed distressed him. Blood must always be available, he thought.

Learning more about blood and how to preserve it for long periods of time was to become Charles Drew's main research interest.

Back home in Washington, D.C., Drew took a teaching position at the Howard University Medical School. He felt that the training of future African-American doctors was the most important contribution he could make to help advance his race in American medicine.

But after only three years, Charles Drew found himself engaged in research again.

The Rockefeller Foundation was offering a research fellowship at New York's Columbia-Presbyterian Medical Center. Dr. Drew was offered the fellowship. It was an easy decision for him to make because the research director of the center, John Scudder, was doing work on blood.

In June 1938, Charles Drew left Washington for New York City. The preservation and storage of blood, still a major problem in medicine, was again his chief concern. In 1937, Dr. Bernard Fantus had opened a blood bank in Chicago. Dr. Fantus had tried to preserve blood on ice.

But the red blood cells still broke down rapidly, releasing the deadly potassium. This made the blood unusable after about 24 hours.

One of the first things that Dr. Scudder and his new research assistant talked about was a blood bank, a place where a person could get the right type of blood immediately. The recipient would repay the blood used by getting friends or relatives to donate blood to the bank. In this way, blood would always be available for others.

The prolonged preservation of blood was the key to successful blood banking. It was the breakdown of red blood cells that spoiled refrigerated blood stored in bottles. (If blood is not handled gently, the red blood cells tend to break down more easily.) Dr. Drew and his staff worked many days and nights studying and experimenting with blood. Blood that was a day old, blood that was seven days old, blood that was several weeks old—these samples were tested on animals.

The refrigeration of carefully handled blood seemed to retard the breakdown of red blood cells. Special containers were designed to keep red cells separated from liquid blood plasma while under refrigeration.

After hundreds of animal tests, it appeared that two-week-old blood was safe for transfusions. Experiments on animals, however, could reveal only so much. How would two-week-old blood react in the human body? What would happen to patients who received two-week-old blood? Dr. Drew decided that these questions would shape his next medical experiment.

Presbyterian Hospital had been considering the establishment of a blood bank for some time. Drew approached Scudder with a bold plan for an experimental blood bank.

Scudder submitted Drew's idea to the medical board of the hospital, which appointed a committee of doctors to study it. Meanwhile, Dr. Drew continued his research.

Finally, the review committee of doctors decided to give an experimental blood bank a four-month trial period. The hospital blood bank was established with Dr. Drew as its medical director.

A New Type of Bank

What was the safest way to preserve blood for transfusions? What was the best way to prevent blood from clotting? What type of container was best for storing blood? These were some of the many questions that needed to be answered.

The first pints of donated blood came from Dr. Drew himself and from the members of his blood bank staff. All of the four types—A, B, AB, and O—were on the blood bank's shelves. In severe emergencies, doctors throughout the hospital called for blood for transfusions. Before and after each transfusion, blood samples from the patient were studied thoroughly.

This close watch over patients who had received blood from the hospital blood bank brought about an important discovery. Blood over a week old appeared to cause some complications to the patient after the transfusion. The red blood cells in blood more than a week old seemed to break down faster than red blood cells in the patient's own blood, a fact that earlier laboratory tests could not have shown. So Dr. Drew had his laboratory technicians throw away any seven-day-old blood.

The blood bank very rapidly proved itself to be an immense success. Dr. Drew's method of preserving blood by careful storage and refrigeration was shown to be safe. He was, however, not satisfied. For one thing, to throw out the seven-day-old blood was a terrible waste. In addition, there were bad reactions in some of the patients who had received whole blood transfusions.

One day, Drew was observing a container of seven-day-old blood, which was about to be thrown away. A layered substance rested on the bottom of the container. Dark red in color, it contained red and white blood cells. A yellowish liquid filled the rest of the container above the layered cells. This straw-colored liquid was blood plasma.

Plasma contains everything that whole blood does, except the blood cells, thought Dr. Drew. And it was the red blood cells that were causing all the trouble. Drew asked himself an important question. Could plasma alone be used safely in transfusions and with the same results as whole blood? Only careful experimentation would give him the answer.

Seven-day-old blood was no longer thrown away. It became a source of plasma. Working with Dr. Scudder and others, Dr. Drew spent many weeks examining plasma in every detail. Plasma did not have to be typed since it did not have red blood cells (the cells that contain the substances that determine the blood types). Plasma was easy to collect. It was found that dried plasma could be stored even more easily and for longer periods of time than liquid plasma. And it didn't have to be refrigerated.

The four-month trial period was coming to an end. Plasma transfusions had to be tried. Drew talked over his plans with Dr. Scudder. In cases where patients didn't need red blood cell replacement, plasma was used.

It worked.

Patients in shock or with severe burns benefited from plasma alone. Dr. Drew had pioneered a breakthrough in medical science and health care. And the work of the new blood bank was allowed to continue beyond the original four-month trial period.

In January 1940, Dr. Drew presented two years of blood research in a thesis called "Banked Blood." Columbia University awarded him a doctor of science degree for his blood research. In this thesis, Dr. Drew discussed the evolution of the blood bank, changes in preserved blood, his own experimental studies in blood preservation, and the·organization, operation, and success of the blood bank at Presbyterian Hospital.

Charles Drew's report was used as a guide in setting up new blood banks in the United States and Europe. By 1940, the Presbyterian Blood Bank had provided patients with 1,800 transfusions. And Dr. Charles Drew had gained national and international fame.

The technique of preparing dried plasma, however, still needed to be perfected. Drew continued experimentation in the use of blood plasma as a substitute for whole blood. In June 1940, his fellowship over, he returned to Howard University to continue his teaching career.

Black Blood

In 1940, World War II was raging in Europe. German planes were attacking and bombing England. Wounded soldiers in hospitals and on the battlefield needed blood badly. The Blood Transfusion Association in New York City offered help. Dr. Drew's old friend from McGill, Dr. John Beattie, was now chief of the Royal Air Force Transfusion Service in England. A cablegram from Dr. Beattie to Dr. Drew at Howard read as follows:

> Could you secure five thousand ampoules dried plasma for transfusion work immediately and follow this by equal quantity in three to four weeks? Contents of each ampoule should represent about one pint whole plasma.

Dr. Drew's return to teaching was interrupted. His research efforts were about to go into action.

The Blood Transfusion Association in New York asked Dr. Drew to come back to New York to help. In the fall of 1940, Drew became medical supervisor of the Blood for Britain Program, a program designed to supply blood for the British Red Cross.

Under Drew's guidance, dried plasma was prepared for airplane shipment to Europe. In October, 5,000 units of dried plasma were flown across the Atlantic to England. Between October 1940 and February 1941, thousands of pints of blood were donated by Americans eager to help the war casualties in Europe. The blood collection and plasma processing techniques worked out by Dr. Drew and his staff were in full use.

Once England had been able to set up its own blood banks, a larger blood program—one intended for the U.S. military forces—was planned. The American Red Cross was to carry out this program at Presbyterian Hospital. Dr. Drew became the director of the first American Red Cross Plasma Bank.

In the spring of 1941, a National Blood Bank Program was being planned for U.S. military men throughout the world. The Blood Transfusion Association and the Red Cross were to carry out this program jointly. Naturally, Dr. Drew was named the medical director of this effort. He was now ready to put his plasma preservation techniques into even wider use.

Dr. Charles Drew had cleared many hurdles during the first 39 years of his life. The first were at track meets. Then came medical school. Developing a safe method of preserving and storing blood plasma for transfusions was the greatest hurdle he faced.

But there was still another obstacle for Charles Drew to clear.

The U.S. armed forces refused to accept blood donations from non-whites to be used by whites. Blood taken by the Red Cross from black donors was to be collected and stored separately—and given only to blacks. Even Dr. Drew's own blood was to be segregated from the blood of white donors.

This was an obstacle that Dr. Drew and his colleagues could not overcome. As a scientist and as director of the Red Cross blood bank program, Dr. Drew gave this statement at a news conference:

> I have been asked my opinion of the practice of separating the blood of Caucasian and Negro donors. My opinion is not important. The fact is that test by race does not stand up in the laboratory.

Charles Drew had taken a strong stand on the racial separation of blood. He resigned his position as director of the Red Cross program and returned once again to teaching at Howard University.

When the Japanese bombed Pearl Harbor in Hawaii on December 7, 1941, plasma was ready. Hundreds of Americans received life-saving plasma transfusions. And Dr. Charles Drew was still contributing to the welfare of his country. He was busy training the young black doctors of the future.

Dr. Drew spent the last years of his life working for the equal treatment of African Americans in every phase of medicine. The practice of segregating blood continued after 1941. Eventually, however, scientific truth won over this form of racial prejudice. And today, blood plasma for transfusions is prepared by pooling blood from people of all races.

Drew predicted that someday whole blood and plasma transfusions would be replaced by more modern methods of blood transfusions. He even dreamed that scientists would create substitutes for the substances making up plasma. The traditional blood bank, he envisioned, would one day be a thing of the past.

A Tragic Accident

On April 1, 1950, Dr. Drew was driving to an annual medical conference at the Tuskegee Institute in southern Alabama. The car he was driving ran off the road and overturned. In the attempt to save his life, Dr. Drew was given plasma. But his injuries were too severe. A blood transfusion could not save his life. He died several hours after the accident. Dr. Charles Drew was 45 years old.

If Charles Drew had lived to the present, he probably would have contributed to the ideas he dreamed so much about. Since his untimely death, much progress has been made in blood science and methods of blood transfusions.

New procedures certainly offer exciting possibilities for the future of medical care. Some scientists believe that it is safer and more successful to give a patient only the blood components (white blood cells, for example). Other scientists are even experimenting with freezing a person's blood. If this works, each person could store some of his or her own blood for an emergency.

Dr. Charles Drew built the foundation for these new efforts in blood research. His work is a permanent and important part of our medical history.

DANIEL HALE WILLIAMS

11

On December 3, 1967, in a hospital in Cape Town, South Africa, Dr. Christian Barnard removed the heart from the body of a woman killed when she was hit by a car. The doctor carried the heart to an adjoining room, where a patient waited for a life-saving operation. Most of this patient's badly diseased heart had already been removed, and a heart-lung machine was pumping blood through his body.

Dr. Barnard proceeded to stitch the dead woman's heart onto the auricles of the man's heart—first the left, then the right. Next, he joined the stub of the aorta of the transplanted heart to the man's aorta. Arteries and veins were connected. Four hours had passed since Dr. Barnard began his heart transplant operation.

Electrodes were attached to each side of the transplanted heart. An electric current was passed to the heart tissue. The heart muscle jumped. The heart began to beat. About an hour later, the man's chest was closed.

Barnard's boldness—and success—stimulated other heart specialists to try this operation. You may have read about the many heart transplant operations carried out throughout the world. Such operations are an established part of medical history.

If we go back to 1893, however, we can find another monumental achievement in the history of medicine and the heart. In that year, the first successful open-heart operation on a human was performed. The operation made an already successful African-American doctor famous.

Daniel Hale Williams was at his hospital in Chicago's black community when a man stabbed in the chest with a knife was brought to the emergency room. The victim's blood pressure began to drop. The pain and coughing of the patient seemed abnormal to Dr. Williams. Perhaps the knife had hit a major blood vessel or even the heart itself, the doctor thought.

The victim's condition worsened overnight; he was bleeding internally. Williams saw that the man was dying.

He decided to operate.

Dr. Williams opened up the man's chest and repaired his wounded heart. He accomplished what most surgical authorities of the time considered both unthinkable and impossible. He was the first surgeon to perform an open-heart operation that saved a human life.

A Chicago newspaper hailed Dr. Williams' pioneering operation with the headline "Sewed Up His Heart." His patient lived for more than 20 years after the operation.

Williams' decision to perform an open-heart operation had been a bold one. Before he performed this famous operation, patients with knife wounds in the chest were treated with rest—and prayers. Dr. Williams' surgery had been skillful. He had studied human anatomy long and hard before the historic operation. Williams' daring—and his success—changed professional and public attitudes about heart surgery.

Living through Hardship

It was only 10 years before his famous open-heart operation that Daniel Williams had received his degree in medicine from the Chicago Medical College. After graduation, Williams was appointed as an instructor in human anatomy at the college, an indication of his exceptional ability in medical science.

For Daniel Williams, medical school was a financial hardship. He had lived through such hardship since the age of 12, when his father died. In his earlier years, however, Dan had been happy and secure.

Dan Williams was born in 1856 as a free black child. His parents were free people living in Pennsylvania at the time of his birth. As a young child, he was able to attend school regularly, which was not the case for most black children at that time in America.

Daniel's father had become a prosperous barber. Mr. Williams was also a strong and active community leader, often speaking about equal rights and opportunities for black people in this country. In 1867, when his father died, Dan's mother was unable to provide for her seven children. Some were sent to live with relatives; others went to a boarding school. Eleven-year-old Dan was left with a shoemaker friend in Baltimore to learn the shoemaking trade. At that point, his schooling ended for a while.

The years that followed were unsettling for young Dan Williams. He had no family or schooling to hold him in one place for long. He moved from job to job. (He even did some barbering.)

But as a teen-ager, Dan recalled what his father had often said: "We colored people must cultivate the mind." These words motivated Dan Williams to get an education.

At 17, Dan was tired of wandering. He went to live with an older sister in Wisconsin. Later, they moved to Janesville, Wisconsin, and it was there that Dan Williams met a well-known black barber named Charles Anderson.

While becoming a barber under Anderson's instruction, Dan found out what he could do with his hands. Handling scissors, combs, and razors helped him to develop good coordination. Cutting hair and shaving men's faces required agile and gentle finger movements. These were also the requirements for a skillful surgeon. (It is interesting to note that in the history of medicine, the first surgeons were barbers. Barbers often performed minor operations in earlier times.)

Working in the barbershop was a kind of school for Daniel Williams. He learned much from listening to his customers' conversations. He borrowed their books and read whenever there was no hair to cut.

College was ever on Dan's mind, and Mr. Anderson allowed him to work part-time so that he could attend high school. Dan arranged for special tutoring, and with this extra help, he was able to graduate in 1877.

A Dr. Palmer frequently came to Anderson's barbershop to get his hair cut. Dan Williams had heard that Dr. Palmer tried to save the life of a man with a gunshot wound. One day, Williams discussed the case with Dr. Palmer as he cut the doctor's hair.

Dr. Palmer's work inspired Dan Williams. He decided that he wanted to become a doctor, too.

Palmer agreed to take Williams on as an apprentice doctor in his office. In those days, working in a doctor's office was the first step in medical training. Dan Williams worked and studied hard under Dr. Palmer. As Dan saw, Dr. Palmer had to work quickly. In the 1800s, surgery was a crude and often brutal business.

After two years, Dr. Palmer felt that his assistants were ready for medical school. His two white apprentices were going to Chicago Medical College, and Dan Williams wanted to go with them. Money was a problem, however. Medical school was expensive. But by working at odd jobs and borrowing some money from Anderson, Williams was able to leave Janesville and enter Chicago Medical College.

Williams often wrote the Andersons to inform them of his progress; they were like foster parents to him. His letters contained requests for money for rent, food, books, tuition, and laboratory fees. His financial plight at times made it hard for Williams to concentrate on his studies in anatomy, physiology, histology, and chemistry. Anatomy was his favorite subject.

The second year of medical school was a bit easier. Summer work had allowed Williams to earn and save some money, and he had regained his health from a bout of sickness during the past spring.

Clinical training in hospitals began during this middle year. Bedside instruction and observing operations were especially exciting to Dan Williams. He was learning about infections, methods of disinfection, and exciting new surgical techniques.

In March 1883, 36 men marched down the aisle of the Chicago Grand Opera House to take the Hippocratic Oath. Dr. Daniel H. Williams was one of them, proud to receive a medical degree from Chicago Medical College.

Discrimination and Dilemma

Dr. Williams decided to stay in Chicago to practice medicine. Black people were migrating by the thousands to Chicago and other northern cities from the South, and

Dr. Williams felt that he would be needed there to serve his people. There were only a few black doctors in Chicago in 1883. Dr. Williams opened his new office on Chicago's South Side, an integrated neighborhood.

Since African-American doctors were not appointed to any hospital staffs, they were unable to work in the white-owned and white-run hospitals. Further, it was difficult for their black patients to gain admission to the few hospitals that were established in Chicago at the time. So when Dr. Williams' patients required surgery, he would perform the operations in the kitchen or dining room of a patient's home or apartment.

Surgery was still largely a trial-and-error procedure for all doctors. But Dr. Williams' operations were quite successful, and his reputation spread rapidly across the city. He started to attract the attention of the entire medical profession in the Chicago area and throughout the state of Illinois.

But Dr. Williams' professional growth was in danger of being stunted. He had little access to further medical training and the newer surgical techniques available to those doctors who were members of white medical groups working in white hospitals. This presented a dilemma for him since he naturally wanted to improve his ability and skills as a doctor and surgeon.

With persistence, Williams gained an appointment to the surgical staff of the South Side Dispensary. This gave him the opportunity to perform minor operations under better conditions than were found in patients' homes. He continued to give instruction in anatomy at Chicago Medical College. In 1889, he was appointed to the Illinois State Board of Health. He served on the board for four years and was a leader in improving medical care and raising health standards for the people of Illinois.

By 1890, several things were distressing Dr. Williams. First, young black women who wanted to become nurses could not gain admission to a nursing school in Chicago. Second, though more young black doctors were graduating each year from medical schools, none could practice in the all-white hospitals. Hospitals, then as now, were the training grounds for doctors and nurses. Third, no hospital was open to Dr. Williams' patients who needed the services that only such a facility could provide. As long as Dr. Williams was not accepted on a hospital staff, he felt, these problems would remain.

Daniel Williams was committed to progress for black people in every phase of medicine—public health, daily medical services, training nurses, training doctors, and providing the best possible surgery. There seemed to be only one solution, a difficult one: Dr. Williams would open his own hospital.

A Different Sort of Hospital

Dr. Williams dreamed of a hospital different from any hospital in America at that time. It was to serve the needs of both white and black people. There would be no more operations done in a dining room or kitchen. While the conditions for black patients, black doctors, and black nurses were foremost in his mind, Dr. Williams felt that his hospital should be open to all people, regardless of their color. His hospital would train and employ white nurses as well as black ones, white doctors as well as black ones. He wanted it to be a hospital for black people, but he did not want a black hospital.

Once Dr. Williams had made up his mind to open his own interracial hospital, he moved quickly. He went to his friends—businessmen, ministers, lawyers, doctors, civic leaders, teachers at Chicago Medical College—both black and white.

Working committees were set up to plan the hospital and to handle the endless details of fund-raising events. Creating a hospital was a heavy burden for Dr. Williams, who still had his own patients to care for each day.

A three-story building was chosen for the hospital site. The floors and walls were scrubbed and painted by volunteers. People donated furniture, sheets, pillows, food, soap, and other necessities. Daniel Williams purchased medical supplies and surgical equipment with some of the money raised for the hospital.

In 1891, the Provident Hospital and Training School Association opened its doors. The hospital had 12 beds. Daniel Williams staffed his hospital with only the most competent doctors. The training program for nurses was rigorous, lasting for 18 months.

In the years ahead, Provident Hospital emerged as a major medical facility. It housed 85 beds and admitted 2,000 patients each year. The emergency room handled more than 9,000 patients annually. The hospital included a pathology laboratory, a physical therapy department, a post-operative recovery room, a social work department, and a pharmacy.

Most of the cases at Provident Hospital during its first two years were surgical. Dr. Williams' ability to diagnose a patient's illness was outstanding. Williams was a keen observer, noting every detail of a patient's condition, and making no diagnosis until he had all of the facts.

At Provident Hospital, Dr. Williams established his remarkable reputation as a surgeon. Doctors from all over the state crowded into his small operating room to watch him perform an operation. His hand motions were quick and smooth, beautiful to watch. Because of his thorough knowledge of human anatomy, he knew what to expect when he cut into tissues and organs.

But before making an incision, Dr. Williams always informed himself of the patient's full medical history. He was ingenious and daring, but never reckless.

It was at Provident Hospital that Daniel Hale Williams performed his famous and pioneering operation.

"Out of Bounds"

Dr. Williams leaned over the chest of a man rushed to Provident Hospital during the evening of July 9, 1893. The victim, James Cornish, had been stabbed close to his heart during a fight near the hospital. Dr. Williams' eyes were steadily fixed on the knife wound in the man's chest. At first, the wound just to the left of the breastbone did not look that serious. The knife had left a cut about an inch long.

At the hospital, the wound had nearly stopped bleeding. It appeared to be superficial. There was no sign of internal bleeding, but there was no way for Dr. Williams to be sure. (There were no X-rays in 1893.) The patient was unable to tell what kind of knife had stabbed him or how long the blade was. With rest, the patient should recover, thought Dr. Williams.

But during the night, Cornish's condition took a turn for the worse. Bleeding started again and continued off and on. The patient had severe pains in the heart area. His pulse weakened; he showed signs of shock. (When a person goes into shock, his blood pressure is at a low point. This is dangerous—it means that the circulatory system is losing blood. Death is a possibility.) The injured man was near collapse.

Perhaps, Dr. Williams thought as he re-examined his patient in the early morning hours, the wound was deeper than he could see.

Dr. Williams knew that something was wrong in the region of the man's heart. But what? Perhaps the knife had punctured or cut a major blood vessel. Perhaps it had struck the heart tissue itself.

James Cornish was growing steadily weaker. It was clear that he was bleeding internally. His wrist pulse could hardly be felt. The pains over the heart and short, sharp coughs persisted. The wounded man was exhausted from a sleepless night.

On the morning following James Cornish's admission to Provident Hospital, Dr. Williams decided to operate. He would open up the left side of the dying man's chest cavity to explore the heart area.

Quickly, he called his staff of doctors and nurses into the hospital's small operating room. Six of Dr. Williams' colleagues were alerted. They crowded into the operating room to watch. The operation began immediately. Nurses were standing by to hand surgical tools to Dr. Williams.

Dr. Daniel Williams worked virtually unaided. He was operating on Cornish in a time before blood transfusions were given, before X-rays were taken. He had no trained anesthetist; he had no drugs to give his patient. There was no heart-lung machine to maintain blood circulation during an operation. Nor was there an electrocardiograph machine to measure electrical impulses from the heart.

Dr. Williams pressed the scalpel point to the bare chest of his limp patient. The first cut was made between two ribs. He lengthened the original wound, making the one-inch stab wound about six inches long.

A second incision was made. This cut exposed part of the breastbone, a portion of a rib near the bone, and some cartilage between the ribs. Next, a small patch of cartilage between the rib and bone was cut, opening a small hole into the chest cavity.

The opening was about two inches long and one and one-half inches wide. The cartilage was difficult to work with since it was elastic in nature and closed up quickly when cut.

Through the opening made in the cartilage, Williams could see some of the major blood vessels. He worked rapidly, tying off and moving blood vessels to make room to get to the heart itself. One of the blood vessels had been pierced by the knife and was leaking blood. Williams tied the injured vessel with catgut to stop the bleeding.

The pericardium—the thin, protective, membranous sac that envelops the heart—was in sight. The sac, too, had received a stroke of the knife blade. The sac wound was about one and one-quarter inches long.

Since the sac tissue lies directly next to the heart, the heart, too, had been hit by the point of the knife blade. The puncture wound in the heart was about one-tenth of an inch long. The heart itself was not bleeding and did not require stitches.

The protective sac around the heart, however, was another matter. The cut in the pericardium would have to be sewn. Dr. Williams flooded the exposed heart area with salt solution to guard against infection.

Then, gently grasping the pericardial tissue with surgical forceps, Williams closed the cut with catgut. He was ready to close up the chest opening. Using silkworm gut, Williams sutured the cartilage and skin incisions made to reach the heart. Finally, a dry dressing was placed over the outside incision.

By the seventh day after the operation, the patient's pulse rate was nearly normal. His fever was down, and his body temperature was back to normal. His heartbeat was strong and regular. About three weeks later, Dr. Williams performed a minor operation to remove some fluid that had collected in Cornish's chest cavity. Eighty ounces of bloody fluid were removed.

Fifty-one days after he was stabbed, James Cornish was released from Provident Hospital. Two years later, Dr. Williams saw his heart patient working hard in a stockyard. For 20 years after his operation, James Cornish lived a normal life.

Daniel Williams was the first man to operate successfully on the human heart. At the time, touching the heart was considered "out of bounds" for surgeons. Even with the best methods of examination available in 1893, it was extremely difficult to diagnose wounds of the pericardium and the heart. In addition, an operation of this sort ran an enormous risk of death from infection.

The reputation and the career of Daniel Hale Williams would have been ruined if his patient had died on the operating table.

"Patient Alive Three Years Afterward"

The historical literature of medicine does not contain a single successful attempt at human heart surgery before 1893. Dr. Williams, however, did not report his work on Cornish until three and one-half years after the operation.

Daniel Williams was delayed in writing and getting his report published earlier because he became ill about the time of Cornish's recovery. Then, upon his own recovery, Dr. Williams accepted a new position as chief surgeon at Freedmen's Hospital in Washington, D.C.

It was not until March 1897 that the *Medical Record*, a weekly journal of medicine and surgery, contained an article titled "Stab Wound of the Heart and Pericardium—Suture of the Pericardium—Recovery—Patient Alive Three Years Afterward."

It was written by Dr. Daniel H. Williams.

In September 1896, Dr. Louis Rehn, a German surgeon, performed a similar heart operation. Rehn's patient had also received a knife-stab wound in the heart. The wound in this patient's heart was larger than the one in Cornish's. In his operation, Dr. Rehn successfully sutured the heart tissue itself.

News of Dr. Rehn's operation spread throughout Germany, Europe, and America. In 1895 and 1896, there were reports from other surgeons who had tried sutures in and around the heart and had failed.

Daniel Williams did not take part in the clamor for recognition, as did Dr. Rehn and other doctors who had tried open-heart surgery. Dan Williams had no time for what he considered foolish disputes about who was the first person to operate on the human heart.

All that Dr. Williams cared about was that he had saved a human life with his heart operation.

In 1908, Dr. Williams celebrated his twenty-fifth year in medicine. Doctors from all parts of the United States gathered in Chicago to honor him at a testimonial dinner. Several years later, he was appointed to the surgical staff at the white St. Luke's Hospital in Chicago. In 1913, he was made a member of the American College of Surgeons.

During the years after his monumental operation, Dr. Williams continued to contribute to the development and improvement of surgery and medical practice. He spoke at medical conventions, wrote articles for medical journals, and helped to train many new surgeons.

"Dr. Dan"

In 1920, Dr. Williams retired to his favorite summer vacation spot on a lake in Idlewild, Michigan, a summer resort town in the northern woods of that state. There, he built a small cottage on a hill overlooking the lake. His well-earned days of rest were spent fishing and caring for his flower garden.

There, too, Daniel Williams became a doctor to anyone in need of medical help. He opened a little hospital for emergencies. He placed a fire bell in a high tower so that he could be called whenever a sick or injured vacationer needed attention.

In 1924, Dr. Williams' wife died, and two years later he suffered a severe stroke. The next five years were sad ones for Dr. Williams. Other strokes followed.

The pain and misery that Dr. Daniel Williams had prevented so many people from experiencing were his to endure during his last years. His was a slow death that could not be helped by medical science. Finally, on August 4, 1931, Dr. Daniel Hale Williams died in Idlewild, the place he loved so much. News stories announced the death of this pioneer surgeon and recounted his medical work and service to people of all races.

Part of a tribute printed in the *Lake County Star*, the paper that served the Idlewild community, read as follows:

His departure from Idlewild was attended with honors and reverence of exceptional character. . . .

It is remarkable that so famous a man should carry his honors so lightly. In 1920, he built his beautiful cottage in Idlewild. . . . He did not practice, but he never turned a deaf ear to a call for help. One of our bankers owes his life to the ministrations of "Dr. Dan," and many others found him willing and ready to serve without pay in the cause of humanity. Modest, retiring, unassuming, he found his little world here full of reverent, loving friends. To the children, he was "Dr. Dan," and a friend even though regarded awesomely as a miracle man.

Like many other truly great men, he found peace, solace, and instruction in nature. He loved his flowers and his garden was filled with lovely plants. He loved the woods and waters and the living things in them. . . .

To have known him was a pleasure—to have known him intimately was a priceless privilege. He was, at once, an inspiration and an aid. To emulate his simplicity, his kindly spirit, and his great modesty is to pay tribute to the truly great. The world has lost greatly.

INDEX

ABOUT THE AUTHOR

An educator, historian, and author, Robert C. Hayden is known nationally for his writing, lecturing, and teaching on the history of African Americans. He is the author of *Black in America: Episodes in U.S. History* (1969) and *African Americans in Boston: More than 350 Years* (1991). He was a contributor to *Dictionary of American Negro Biography* (1982). From 1974 to 1983, his weekly column, "Boston's Black History," appeared in the *Bay State Banner* in Boston. In 1986, he wrote a viewer's guide to the television series "Eyes on the Prize: America's Civil Rights Years, 1954 to 1965."

Hayden's first biography for young readers, *Singing for All People: Roland Hayes*, was published in 1989. His other books include *Faith, Culture and Leadership: A History of the Black Church in Boston*; *Boston's NAACP History: 1910 to 1982*; and *The African Meeting House in Boston: A Celebration of History.*

A member of the Executive Committee of the Association for the Study of Afro-American Life and History and president of the Boston branch of the association, Hayden is also a lecturer in the Department of African-American Studies at Northeastern University and in the Black Studies Program at Boston College. In addition, he holds adjunct faculty positions at Bentley College and Curry College.

Hayden is president of RCH Associates, an educational consulting firm that works with school and community groups to develop awareness of African-American life and history and to foster intergroup understanding and communication.

Hayden served as executive director of the Massachusetts Pre-Engineering Program from 1987 to 1991.

From 1980 to 1982, Hayden was employed by the Boston Public Schools, where he held several administrative positions: special assistant to the superintendent, executive assistant to the superintendent, and director of project development. He also served as director of the Secondary Technical Education Project at the Massachusetts Institute of Technology.

From 1970 to 1973, he served as executive director of the Metropolitan Council for Educational Opportunity in Boston and then worked in educational research and development at the Educational Development Center in Newton, Massachusetts.

During the early years of his career, Hayden was a science teacher, a news writer for *Current Science*, and a science editor in the educational division of Xerox Corporation.

Hayden earned his B.A. in 1959 and a master's degree in 1961, both from Boston University. He has also completed two post-graduate fellowships: one in the School of Education at Harvard University (1965-1966), the other in the Department of Urban Studies and Planning at the Massachusetts Institute of Technology (1976-1977).

Robert Hayden is the author of three volumes in "Achievers: African Americans in Science and Technology." This biography series includes *11 African-American Doctors*, *9 African-American Inventors*, and *7 African-American Scientists*. First published in the 1970s, these books have now been revised, expanded, and updated by the author.